OVER THE BAR

MEMORIES OF MY CAREER WITH
ARSENAL F.C. & WALES

By
JACK KELSEY

As told to Brian Glanville

GCR BOOKS
www.gcrbooks.co.uk

With thanks to
Peter Kelsey and Paul Kelsey
for their kind cooperation in the
republication of their father's book.

Special thanks also to
Brian Glanville
for his consent and support for this project.

First Published in Great Britain 1958 by Stanley Paul

This edition published 2011 by GCR Books Ltd - www.gcrbooks.co.uk
ISBN 978-0-9559211-6-2

Copyright © Jack Kelsey & Brian Glanville 1958
Foreword © Greg Adams 2011

Cover image courtesy of Mirrorpix.com
Cover design by GCR Books Ltd
Text and editing by Greg Adams

All rights reserved. No reproduction, copy or transmission of this publication may be made without written permission or in accordance with the provisions of the Copyright, Design and Patents Act 1988 (as amended). Any person who does any unauthorized act in relation to this publication may be liable to criminal prosecution and civil claims for damages.

This book is sold subject to the condition that it shall not, by way of trade or otherwise, be lent, resold, hired out, or otherwise circulated without the publisher's prior consent in any form of binding or cover other than that in which it was published and without a similar condition including this condition being imposed on the subsequent purchaser.

Printed and bound in Great Britain by Lonsdale Print Solutions, Wellingborough.

FOREWORD

The image of Alfred John "Jack" Kelsey adorns the façade of the Emirates Stadium alongside 31 other Arsenal legends with the majority of these 32 players belonging to periods in the Club's history filled with league titles and cup final glory. Not so for Jack Kelsey. After 14 years at Highbury, he had only one league championship medal to show for his 352 club appearances. To have achieved "legend" status during such a lean period speaks volumes about his contribution to Arsenal Football Club and his ability as a goalkeeper.

Only three goalkeepers appear on the mural, the other two being the 1970's great, Bob Wilson, and David Seaman, arguably the Club's most successful keeper and the only goalkeeper to have made more Arsenal appearances than Kelsey. Excellent company indeed.

Inevitably, Jack Kelsey was also to receive international recognition and was capped 41 times for his country between 1954 and 1962. These caps included Wales' sole appearance in the World Cup Finals, in 1958, when they qualified through the back door after beating Israel in a two-leg play-off. The much maligned and unfancied Welsh team silenced their critics by reaching the quarter-finals, where a deflected shot from 18-year-old Pele resulted in a 1-0 victory for Brazil and an end to Welsh World Cup dreams.

Despite the disappointment in Sweden, Kelsey had secured his place in the annals of Welsh football history too. If the Millennium Stadium had a mural of Welsh legends you'd find his image there as well.

Greg Adams
GCR Books

CONTENTS

Chapter	Page
1. A Nightmare Beginning.	1
2. Almost a Guardsman.	9
3. "Are you a Goalkeeper?"	23
4. Arsenal's Telephone Jokers.	39
5. League Champions.	63
6. Confetti and Red Dragons.	80
7. Retreat from Moscow.	95
8. A Lesson from Europe.	110
9. Red Dragons Triumphant.	128
10. The Passing of Tom Whittaker.	143
11. Welsh Wembley – and a World Cup Exit.	146
12. A Scottish Pound Note.	166
13. Why not Britain?	182
14. Arsenal under Fire.	187
15. Reprieve for Wales.	192
16. Wales go to Sweden.	197

1
A NIGHTMARE BEGINNING

I didn't know I'd be playing until I looked over someone's shoulder at an evening paper, while travelling on the underground railway. There unmistakably was my picture, and it could only be there for one reason. Looking quickly up the page at the headline, I read, sure enough, that I was "likely" to make my debut in goal for Arsenal that Saturday, against Charlton Athletic.

"I must buy that paper as soon as I get out of the tube," I told myself – and did so. The text had little more to tell me; after all, this was Tuesday, still early in the week. Tuesday 17 February, 1951. "Jack Kelsey," said the paper, "Arsenal's young Welsh goalkeeper, *may* make his league debut on Saturday."

Good-oh, I thought. Perhaps I'll play, perhaps I won't, but at least it's a start to say that you *may* be playing.

Seeing it in the papers had been a shock. With George Swindin, the regular Arsenal keeper, still injured, and Ted Platt, his deputy, not showing the best of form at the time, I knew I must have some slight chance of coming in – but not necessarily for this game. And besides, this seemed all against club policy, which was firmly based on the tenet that players should be the first to learn of any such decision, whether it regarded their promotion to a team, or their omission. But if I did get picked, I thought, at least this was a nice, easy game to begin with. Charlton were struggling against relegation at the time, and there was real danger of their going down.

Calculating like this was a mistake on my part. If I did not know then, I was very soon to learn that there is no such thing as pure soccer logic in a London "derby" match.

Next morning, when I reported as usual for training at the Arsenal Stadium, I was unconsciously distracted, waiting for a call to Tom Whittaker's office. It came, and there was the Boss, shirt-sleeved behind his desk, as usual, the Great White Father of the club, the manager revered by everyone at Highbury.

"I suppose you read the papers last night," he said, in his comfortable north-eastern accent.

"As a matter of fact," I replied, "I did."

"It shouldn't have been in," said Whittaker, "it's against club policy. But it doesn't matter: you're in. You are playing against Charlton." I mumbled something about being delighted. "Play your normal game," he said, "and keep your eye on the ball." I promised I would. Oddly, it was the only technical advice that the Boss would ever give me.

All the boys at Highbury were very nice about it, but nicest of all was the man whose place I had taken; Ted Platt, the burly, unofficial club comedian, who had been on the Arsenal books while I was still in short trousers.

He was standing in the boot-room, directly opposite to me as I came out of the dressing-room, and he stopped me. "Look, son," he said, "you can make this position your own. Keep it." It seemed to me a wonderful gesture.

When I arrived home at my cousin's house in Romford, he congratulated me, and told me that he'd make the extreme sacrifice. Although he was a West Ham supporter and had been for years, this week he would be at Highbury to watch the Arsenal! Then I sat down and wrote a letter to my parents, in Winch Wen. I was very happy, of course, but I had no illusions about being "arrived". I had made it, to the extent of being picked for league football, but I hadn't yet proved myself. My family, however, were thrilled enough to send me a wire. They would not be seeing the match, though, since they had already arranged to come up to London for Easter. I hoped that I would still be in the side by then.

Late on Saturday morning, I reported at the Great Northern Hotel, King's Cross, for lunch with the rest of the team; the customary steak and toast. We seemed to be taking it all rather lightly, in view of Charlton's low position in the table, and the Boss did not go into the game in any great detail, at the preliminary talk. He did, however, advise us to "watch Jeppson", but perhaps we did not heed him sufficiently.

Certainly the advice was well grounded. Hans (or Hasse, to give him his real name) Jeppson was well known to all of us by now for his feats in recent weeks. The previous year, he had played a great part in the Swedish World Cup team which reached the Final Pool in Rio, scoring a couple of goals, to knock out Italy. Now he was in England, studying the manufacture of office furniture, and turning out for Charlton at centre-forward, as an amateur. Lately, he had been banging in the goals which gave Charlton narrow and life-saving wins. In his very first match, he had got the winner at home to Sheffield Wednesday. Nevertheless, Jeppson or no Jeppson, we felt confident enough.

These were the teams that took the field at Highbury on a brisk February afternoon:

Arsenal: Kelsey, Barnes, L. Smith, Shaw, L. Compton, Forbes, McPherson, Logie, Goring, Lewis, Roper.

Charlton Athletic: Bartram, Croker, Lock, Fenton, Phipps, Hewie, Hurst, Evans, Jeppson, Vaughan, Kiernan.

I'd been playing solo at the hotel until it was time to leave, and had been suffering with the inevitable butterflies in the stomach. I kept thinking to myself, if I can make a good save early in the match, I shall be all right. But when I trotted out of the tunnel to face the biggest crowd in front of which I had ever played, I was not specially put out. For some reason, crowds – British crowds – have never bothered me much.

Looking down at the other goal, two heads attracted my attention; one red, one blond. The red hair belonged to Sammy Bartram, who had been in Charlton's goal for the past seventeen years, a giant among goalkeepers, both physically and metaphorically. The fair, curly hair was that of Hasse Jeppson, the Swede who had been terrorizing First Division goalkeepers. I noticed the easy power with which he right-footed the ball at goal.

Within minutes, the game had begun, and almost at once my wish was fulfilled. Billy Kiernan, on the Charlton left-wing, sent over a fast cross, about head high. I had my eye on it firmly from the start, moved out at the right moment, and held it firmly and easily. Good-oh, I thought, at least I didn't drop the first one. I began to settle down a bit. As for Jeppson, I thought, Big Les will take care of him; after all, hadn't Compton been England's centre-half in their last two matches? It turned out, alas, to be a false equation.

After about eighteen minutes, in which Arsenal had seemed to be getting a grip on the game, Charlton suddenly scored. Fair-haired Gordon Hurst beat Lionel Smith out on the right wing, and cut in towards goal. If Arsenal's traditional, interlocking defence had been functioning as it should have done, either Big Leslie Compton or Walley Barnes – or both – would have been there to provide cover. Instead, Hurst was given a clear path. He shot from some twelve yards out, in line with the corner of the penalty box. I made an effort to reach the ball, but it was a vain one. It was some tiny consolation to see next morning's papers say that I hadn't a chance. I must say it didn't seem like it, at the time.

That was the beginning, but a second goal came along which really put Charlton on top – and should never have been allowed; a naughty goal, I felt. Hurst crossed the ball, Arthur Shaw shaped to head it away, when suddenly one of the Charlton players standing by him, yelled, "Leave it!" Arthur did, and the player promptly banged the ball into the net. We looked on, open-mouthed, as the referee pointed to the centre-spot.

Peter Goring made the score 2-1, and things began to look a little better, but it was then that Hasse Jeppson came into the game. The first of his goals came when he rounded Leslie Compton with surprising ease, and neatly placed his shot. The pace wasn't very great, so that the agony of diving for the ball, only to see it just elude me, was all the greater. The shot clipped the upright, and went in, making us 3-1 down at half-time.

Tom Whittaker came massively into the dressing room to say, "You're taking this game too lightly. Pull yourselves together, take a grip on yourselves! Get out there for the second half and give them some of their own medicine!" Which we failed to do.

Indeed, to my dismay and despair, it wasn't long before Charlton had increased their lead to 4-1. Jeppson again, getting the better of Compton, and sending the ball home with a well-placed shot which I could not reach, painfully as I tried.

Again there was a flicker of hope when Peter Goring scored his and Arsenal's second goal, to make the score 2-4, but once more, Jeppson torpedoed it, and what a humiliating goal it was! Leslie Compton tried to pass back from far out, misjudged his kick, and Jeppson was around him once again, like an eel, with the goal at his mercy. I advanced to meet him, but "Hans" is too good a centre-forward to miss chances like that. We had lost, 5-2. A more miserable goalkeeper never slunk off Arsenal's pitch; not even Spain's great Zamora, when he let through seven against England. I wasn't there at the time, but I know he could not have been unhappier than I was. And the odd thing about the match was that, apart from his three good goals, it seemed to me that Jeppson did not accomplish a great deal.

"Bad start, good finish," I said to myself. It wasn't much, but it was the only consolation that I could think of. And I needed all that I could get when I found out that it was the first time for twenty-five years that Arsenal had let through as many goals at home. A quarter of a century, I thought, and when it happened, they had to pick my match. The depression which I had been feeling ever since the first goal grew deeper still. Truthfully speaking, I did not feel that I had had much chance with any of the goals, but the fact remained that there had been five of them, and it was my debut.

The unkindest cut of all was reserved for that night, when I came out of a local cinema, in an unsuccessful attempt to forget my sorrows. I emerged at about a quarter past ten and went down the tube at Finsbury Park. Standing on the platform waiting for the train, I saw two men talking to one another and looking at me. When I applied my attention, I could hear that they were discussing whether or not I was Jack Kelsey. At last one of them came over to me and asked, "Are you Kelsey?"

I didn't want to admit it. At the moment, I would rather have been almost anyone else. At last I mumbled, "I suppose so."

"Thanks, mate," was the reply. "I'm a Charlton supporter."

That sunk me like a torpedo salvo. I was only too ready to feel guilty, and this made me think that perhaps it had all been my fault. That night it was hours before I got to sleep. I was playing the game over and over again in my mind, brooding on every Charlton goal.

When the Sunday papers arrived the next morning, they cheered me up a bit. It was true that one paper carried a banner, NIGHTMARE DEBUT FOR KELSEY, but the reports were all very kind and fair to me. I'd been slated by nobody, and now that I had a chance to reflect, I remembered that everyone had been pretty nice about it at Highbury, too. First into the dressing-room afterwards had been my old pal Len Wills who had been watching from the stand. He'd made a bee-line towards me as I sat there, me head on my knees, the most lonely and miserable young man in London. "Never mind, Jack," he'd said, "it wasn't your fault," and later, members of the side had consoled me with similar words. Back at home, my West Ham supporting cousin had told me, "From what I could see, you weren't to blame," and I knew that he had been watching football for a long time.

Nevertheless, it needed the tolerance of the Press to set me to rights again. It can't be true, I had been telling myself; and then, with exaggeration perhaps pardonable in a youngster, "It's another Walsall. Charlton – struggling at the bottom of the table. It should have been a cakewalk." Which in retrospect seems to me a good lesson that no game at all should ever be taken lightly.

What gave me most hope of all was a reporter's quote from the Boss, Tom Whittaker. "Kelsey," he had said, "is like a pilot who has crashed on his first flight. He must be sent up again at once so that he regains his confidence."

And sure enough, when I reported for training on Monday, Tom sent for me to say, "What I put in the paper was quite true. You'll be there against Manchester United, next Saturday." It was the best and kindest gesture he could have made.

But one more stab was reserved for me, before I could start forming scar tissue over the wounds left by this unlucky match. The following morning, some of the boys who had been to Finsbury Park Empire for the Monday evening show (it's a tradition for us players to get free passes) told me that I'd been made the butt of Old Mother Riley. Apparently at one point in the performance, Mother Riley's "stooge" had come on to the stage wearing tattered clothes, and with the dead white face of a corpse.

Arthur Lucan, alias Mother Riley, had asked, "Who are you?"

"I'm so and so," was the reply, to which Lucan responded, "For a minute, I thought you were Arsenal's new goalkeeper." It didn't get much of a laugh, I was told.

Nevertheless, I thought it was a bit unfair after my first match; twisting the knife in the wound. I went upstairs to complain to the Governor, who said that he would see to it. He was as good as his word, for the joke wasn't in the show again that night – or any other.

2
ALMOST A GUARDSMAN

Coincidence plays a part in everybody's life, I suppose, but I still say it's had more than its fair share in mine. If my birthday hadn't fallen on 19 November, I'd have signed on for five years in the Welsh Guards, and that would probably have been the end of professional football for me. If, on the other hand, I'd agreed to turn up on time to a relative's birthday party, I would probably never have joined the Arsenal. But I'm racing ahead. Everything in its own place; stories should begin at the beginning, and mine began unspectacularly in Winch Wen.

Winch Wen is a tiny village in the south of Wales. When I was born nearby at Llansamlet, it was not much more than a collection of shops and houses, centred around two intersecting roads, but Swansea was only three and a half miles to the south-east. My father, who was to play so big a part in starting me on the road that led to pro football, was not a Welshman at all.

He is, in fact, a Cockney, but his family moved from London when he was fourteen years old, and he was happy enough to stay in Wales, and to marry a Winch Wen girl – my mother. He worked as a smelter furnace-man in a Swansea factory, but efficient though he was, and is, at his job, his heart was elsewhere. Though he had never played regular, organized football in his life, most of his spare time was given to the affairs of the Winch Wen football club, and his short, sturdy, bustling figure was a focal point in the committee, of which he was eventually chairman for twelve years.

And that was how I was initiated into football; as an "honorary" member of the committee, and surely the youngest they had ever had. Even as a toddler, my father would bring me into meetings and sit me on his knee. At the age of five, I became the club mascot. A few years after that, I was actually joining the players on their training runs – and beating half of them, too!

One of those runs produced a painful experience, which I still recall. We were running through the village, and I was well up with the leaders – for that was one thing I could do as a ten year old; run. Suddenly the man who was running directly in front of me swerved. All my concentration was directed to keeping up with him, and I carried straight on – into a lamp-post. That put a stop to my training for a while.

When I began school, it was in the village of Cwm, three- quarters of a mile or so away, a village even smaller than Winch Wen. I can hardly say I learned my football there, for I can only remember having three games, for the school junior team, before the war put an end to organized soccer.

Though I was only eleven years old, all those games were in goal, for I seem to be one of those goalkeepers who are fated from the beginning to stand under the bar. It wasn't a question of choice – goalkeeping was simply forced upon me. In the pick-up games which we village boys used to organize, I was considered too small to play in the field, so they shoved me in goal to keep me out of the way. I've often reflected since that goal is a funny place to seek safety, but I do plead not guilty to the charge that goalkeepers are crazy. I wasn't crazy enough to become a goalkeeper because I wanted to.

Winch Wen, I should add, was by no means a typically Welsh village. My father was far from being the only "foreigner", for there were many others born outside Wales, among them a number of Irishmen. No Welsh was spoken at all, and neither my two sisters (one is younger than I, the other

10

older) not I ever found ourselves the odd children out because we did not know the language.

At the age of twelve, a frightening accident nearly cost me all chance of a soccer career. It was one of those accidents which suddenly arise when you suspect no danger at all. A young friend of mine and I found some sections of a Nissen hut, which had not been put up, yet. Water lay in the corrugated runnels, but we decided to shake it out and improvise a see-saw. This we did by turning one section upside-down on top of the other.

"You lift up," said my friend, "while I press down."

I obeyed him, bending over the sheet of iron. At that moment he pressed down sharply on his side, and the "see-saw" sprang up to hit me in the face. It caught me so violent a blow as to knock me unconscious, giving me a great, diagonal wound across the face, whose scar I bear on my nose to this day. Together with my worried friend, I made my way, not to my home, but to the local ambulance man.

He was something of a legend with us kids. Officially, he was medical officer at my father's factory; unofficially, he looked after us, as well. When we had cuts and bruises needing treatment, we would always go to him, rather than risk the inevitable scolding at home. This time, he was as kind and efficient as ever, but my mother had the shock of her life when I suddenly appeared, my face and head heavily bandaged. It was a narrow escape.

During the war, my football was confined to the village. I remember one day looking up, fascinated, when an aeroplane passed over. In our little village, in the wilds of Wales, aeroplanes were still something pretty exciting at that time. But alas for me, the rest of the boys went on playing. Somebody shot at goal, my attention was attracted just in time, and I luckily managed to save. That taught me a lesson, anyway; keep your eye and your mind on the game.

One thing I did manage to do, throughout the war, was to watch Swansea Town; my father would regularly take me. There were some fine players to watch at the time, the sort of footballers who would stimulate any youngster's interest in the game. Ernie Jones, for example, a young outside-right, then, who had joined the club from Bolton Wanderers. I don't think Ernie has ever played any better than during the war years. He was a wonderful ball player, and very, very fast. Later, of course, he joined the Spurs, and passed on from there to Southampton and Bristol. But I'm sure he never produced quite the same brilliant form he showed those days, at Vetch Field.

Another of my Swansea idols, in those war and immediate post-war years, was Trevor Ford. Trevor was all go then, a player who never stopped moving around, the kind of centre-forward who must have been a terror to opposing third backs. I remember that during the season in which he hit home forty-one goals, I never missed a home match.

Another Swansea star who commanded my admiration was Roy Paul – who stayed with them, of course, till 1950. Roy's wing-half-back play was sheer joy. He played like an artist, and everything about his game was stylish. The ball seemed to flow from him, and I specially admired the way he pulled it down with his chest.

But as an aspiring goalkeeper, most of my attention was naturally given to the man between Swansea's posts; a guest player, Fred Standbridge. Fred was a much more than useful performer, and the thing which left the greatest impression on me was his habit of making a mark. Regularly, before each match, he would stalk out to the six yard line, and dig a tiny pit with his heel. Why did he do it, I wondered, and tried hard to work it out for myself. At last, after a good many weeks of puzzling, I had it. He wanted to be sure of gauging his distance, for intercepting the high crosses. Ever since then, I have always made a heel mark myself, and have become so used to it that I'm sure I would feel quite lost without it.

There was many a good game in the South-West Regional League to which Swansea were consigned for most of the war, and others, even better, in the 1945-6 transitional season. Yet I must admit that only one stands out in my memory, and that not on account of the brilliant football played, but because it featured the biggest goal-mouth scrimmage I've ever seen or been in, in my life.

The opposition was Reading, and I seem to remember that their goalkeeper was the old Arsenal star, George Marks, a Highbury predecessor. Roy Paul took a penalty kick, which Marks saved. Roy, following up, sent the keeper staggering into the net, and that was the signal for a remarkable scrum, in which everyone except Swansea's goalie seemed to join. Within seconds, the net was full of players as a trawler's net in a herring school is full of fish. It was minutes before the confusion was sorted out, and then the referee gave a free kick for a foul on the goalkeeper. Perhaps that should have warned me about persevering in the role myself, but it didn't.

The odd thing was that my secret, cherished dream was to keep goal for....Huddersfield Town. I cannot explain why, for explanation is beyond me. I had never seen Huddersfield play. It is doubtful if I could have told you the names of more than one or two players in their team. Swansea with Paul and Ford – players with whom, unknown to me, I was destined to represent my country – was my beloved side. And yet it was Huddersfield I wanted to go to. No doubt a spot of "free association" on the psychologist's leather couch would bring one to the truth, but in the meanwhile, I am still as baffled as anybody.

It wasn't even as though the Huddersfield Town goalkeeper, Bob Hesford, was a particular hero of mine. Far from it; for me, there was only one goalkeeper in the world, and he "kept" for little Winch Wen.

His name was Staddon, and we always knew him as Billo. Billo was one of those many players whose potentially fine careers were torpedoed by the war. Although, as a boy, I may have exaggerated my hero-worshiping a little, looking back, I know that he was a splendid keeper. He was very small for the position, somewhat similar to Swansea and Ipswich's Welsh international, Jack Parry, in build, but his size did not make any difference to him. To compensate for it, he had tremendous agility, and he reminded one of a cat. He was immensely daring, and his lack of inches did not alter the fact that he could pick the crosses out of the air with great ease and skill. As far as I was concerned, you could keep your Bartrams and your Swifts; Billo Staddon was the only goalkeeper for me.

How far he would have gone if it was not for the war can now be only a matter for speculation. He was about twenty-three when he went into the army, and quite ready, as far as I could judge, to step into a good league team. Certainly he was the top goalkeeper of that time in the Swansea and District League.

When I was fourteen years old I left school and went to work. I had wanted to be a carpenter. As a kid, I had always beguiled the time by chipping-up wood. But when it came to the point, I preferred to stay with the rest of the lads from Winch Wen, most of whom at that time were employed in a Swansea tinplate works. For eighteen months, I was employed in making the tin, first of all as partner to a tin cutter. His job was to slice up the tin with a pair of shears. Mine was to gather the pieces together and send it away for scrap. It was good work, but dangerous, for one collected a great many scratches and cuts. After six months of this, I changed to something a good deal more arduous. I was filling out by now, so they put me on to what was strictly a man's job – actually making the tin. To do this involves getting a slab of steel, and putting it into the furnace. Then it must be passed through the roller, where, while it is still red hot, a man bends it and presses it down into two pieces. Back into the furnace it goes again and the process is repeated, until you eventually get eight pieces. My function in all this was to pull the steel slab out of the roller and push it back to be rolled again. It was very definitely man's work, a heavy job which quickly built up my physique. But I was still only a youngster. I developed pains in my chest, had frightening visions of a weak heart, and decided to give the job up.

No sooner said than done. I walked out there and then, and neither my father nor my mother, both of them on holiday at the time, knew anything about it, until they returned. By that time, they found me in a new job.

It was that of a crane driver. "I'm not going to wait," I told myself, and took the first interesting work that was offered to me. I soon picked up the idea of how to work the crane, which was used for the lifting of red-hot tubes. Alas, this job had its disadvantages, too. It had to be carried out a great deal nearer to heaven than any job I have had before or since, with the result that it was very hot indeed during the summer, and bitterly cold in winter. So high up was it that I could never work during the winter months, without an overcoat, and sometimes I even had to wear two. I stuck out the uncomfortable conditions for as long as I could, for the work itself was pleasant enough. Then I left and, at the age of sixteen and a half, took my third job, leaving the mill in which, as I was to discover, Ray Daniel was also employed for a time.

Now, to my delight, I was able to join my father's factory, which was the nearest of all to Winch Wen. My job was another good one, that of painting and rigging. The rigging side of it entailed fixing your own tackle; ropes, hoists, and the rest of it, and it meant learning another rather technical business. I had been in the Boy Scouts, which helped a little so far as mastering the relevant knots was concerned – but only a little. I was the youngest of the painting-rigging crew, and they started me gently on the easy jobs, painting girders ten feet off the ground, using small tackles. Then I graduated to making my own chairs, and before long I was high aloft again – but not as uncomfortably high as I was in my crane.

Meanwhile, from the age of fifteen, I had been playing in goal for Winch Wen Juniors; it made a change from the friendly, fifteen-a-side affairs which were as near as I came to organized football, during the war. Billo Staddon was back from the army and took up his place again with the first team. To me, he looked almost as good as ever.

My own great ambition at the time was to play on Vetch Field, hallowed as it was by the feet of Roy Paul, Trevor Ford and Ernie Jones. But for the moment at least, the ambition wasn't destined to be gratified. When Winch Wen Juniors seemed on the point of playing their way to Swansea, our local Wembley, something always happened to stop us. Twice we were knocked out in the semi-finals of the Swansea and District Junior Cup. I didn't play at Vetch Field until I came down with the Arsenal combination team.

It wasn't till 1947, the year I joined the army, that I at last got my chance in the senior team of Winch Wen. Billo Staddon, with whom it had been a thrill to train, was very nice about it. "All the best," he said. "You keep the place, and good luck to you." But in the event, I had only eleven games.

I wasn't dropped. In all modestly, I think I could have kept my place. But the Juniors were short of a goalkeeper and I was politely asked if I would mind going back, for the rest of the season. I readily agreed. Billo Staddon, though getting on a little, now, proved perfectly capable of filling his old place with his old distinction.

Playing in the Juniors did give me one experience for which I was grateful: I was able to bump a goalkeeper!

The opportunity arose a few months before my call-up. Winch Wen had picked up a young goalkeeper, and were anxious to try him. Accordingly, I played in goal for the first half of a game, then went to centre-forward, while he took over my jersey. I don't remember doing anything brilliant, but I do remember having a vigorous go at the opposing goalkeeper. Seeing football from the other fellow's point of view, I felt at the time...

Not long after that, and still with vague hopes of one day keeping for Huddersfield, at the back of my mind, I reported for my army medical. I passed A1, at Swansea, and was asked what regiment I would like to join. I said that I thought that I wanted to go into the Welsh Guards.

Now, there was a good reason for this. A friend of our family was Police Constable Butler, who, looking at my frame, built up by work in the steel mill, remarked one day that I would make a good policeman. I found the idea quite attractive, and the constable suggested it would be a good thing if I first served in the Guards as a sort of foundation.

Thus, I was taken along to the recruiting officer, who seemed quite enthusiastic about the idea. "Yes," he said, "by all means," and he gave me all the necessary information. There was one snag. He wanted me to report at Caterham on 17 November, and my birthday was on the 19th; I was to be eighteen years old. "If it's all the same to you," I told him, "I'd like to spend that day at home." The officer said that this was quite agreeable to him. I added, remembering my father's warning never to sign anything at all, without consulting him, "I would like to get my parents' consent first."

The officer replied that this was quite in order, too. He even gave me an escort all the way home, in the shape of a recruiting sergeant. The sergeant was very persuasive, as such sergeants always are. He told me all about what a wonderful life I was going to enjoy in the army. "Carpentry?" he said. "You're interested in carpentry? Oh, there's plenty of carpentry in the Welsh Guards," which no doubt there was. When he heard that my chief interest of all was soccer, he became positively ecstatic.

"There are wonderful opportunities for football," he assured me."

At home, my father was not displeased at the idea. "Yes," he said, "join up, if you want to." The recruiting sergeant went off, happy at the thought that another Welsh Guard had been found, and I prepared to spend my last few days of civilian life as pleasantly as possible.

But then I began to think about what I had done – or had promised to do. I must sign on for five years, and five years seemed a terribly long time. I started to brood, and the result of my brooding was that I suddenly decided against it. I was not going to join the Welsh Guards. There and then I sat down to express my decision to the recruiting officer.

Thus it was that I did not go into the army until the time arrived for my National Service. Together with an old classmate, Ronnie Morse, I reported at Wrexham for my basic training, and I remember that my first impressions were not too good. Indeed, the first thing I saw was a squad of recruits busily sweeping the snow off the barrack square. "That's one job I'm not going to like," I said to myself.

It was a dreary few weeks. I believe I spent most of my free time copying caricatures of famous soccer stars, then having a try at drawing them free-hand, myself, and so far as I recall, the results were fairly good. But it was just a way of killing time, for I had no intention of becoming a cartoonist, as Jimmy Seed did in his Tottenham days, I'm told. After a while, we were moved from our freezing cold wooden huts to brick barracks across the way, and life became a good deal less uncomfortable. There wasn't much football, though; half a match was my ration. Nor did I distinguish myself.

I happened to be watching a game, in which one of the goalkeepers had to leave at half-time, to go on duty. I volunteered to take his place, forgetting in my eagerness to handle a football again that age-old army maxim that one should never volunteer for anything. Still dressed in denims and my army boots, I went into goal, football starved, a month in camp without so much as seeing a ball. I must have been out of touch as well as practice, or perhaps the other side just staged a rally. At any rate, our team's 3-0 lead melted away until, by the final whistle, we were losing 4-3. That did not make me very popular.

Not long after that, I was posted to Guillimont Barracks, Farnborough, in the Royal Engineers – as a painter and rigger. I cannot pretend that I ever enjoyed army life very much, but life at Guillimont could have been worse. With the exception of a couple of unpleasant brushes with the sergeant-major, it was certainly better than basic training. But one great disadvantage persisted – there was no opportunity for football.

It was true that the camp had a team. In it played a robust, dark-haired young back called....Cliff Holton. Cliff was already an Arsenal pro, having joined them from Oxford City, and I need hardly say that it never occurred to me at that time that I would one day be joining him.

Still, seeing the camp play was all very well, but I have never been one for exercise by proxy, and I wanted a game myself. Since it became apparent that nobody was going arrange one for me, I took matters into my own hands. Picking out a couple of other young soccer enthusiasts, I said, "Let's fix a soccer match tomorrow with the hut across the road." They needed no urging, and nor did our opponents. We drew boots at the stores, and buckled down to it, though some of us had never played the game before, in our lives.

My side lost again, but this time I had my excuse, for we went down 6-5 – thanks to half a dozen own goals. Nevertheless, I enjoyed it as much as any thirsty explorer in the desert would enjoy a drink of water.

It was indirectly thanks to this game that I had my first brush with the sergeant-major, and most unpleasant it was. I had suffered a kick on the knee, and the following morning I decided to report sick. Together with a couple of my hut companions I made my way to the M.O. As we marched down the side of the barrack square, the R.S.M. and an officer were just coming off, and we acknowledged them with what seemed to me to be a most unexceptionable salute.

The R.S.M., an enormous Scot known familiarly as "the Pig", and to me always a figure of nightmare, called us back. I wondered what on earth was wrong. Perhaps we were out of step, for my injured knee meant that I was hobbling. But back we came, on we marched again – only to hear another bellow, "You there on the end!"

That might have been me or the other fellow, and I sincerely hoped it wasn't me. Both of us looked round, but to my dread, I saw that the R.S.M.'s baton was pointing straight at me. "*You*!" he roared.

I hobbled uncomfortably back to him. "What's that?" he snarled, pointing at a tiny hole in the trouser leg of my denims. I knew of its existence, but it seemed hardly noticeable, and I had postponed doing anything about it. The R.S.M., alas, did not think it ought to be there.

Indeed he went so far as to shove his baton into the hole, rip the trouser leg all the way up, then all the way down. So there I was, stranded on the barrack square, with the leg of my torn denims flapping in the wind like some battered banner. "You'll be out on a charge!" he shouted. "Go and wait in my office!"

I limped my way there, and prepared, in trepidation, to wait. A sergeant arrived, and grinned when he saw my predicament. "What happened?" he asked, and when I explained, he said, "He must be in a hell of a bad temper. Quick! Get off before he catches you."

I needed no persuading. Despite my knee, I was off like Stanley Matthews at his fastest, to draw another pair of denims. Luckily there was only about another week to serve in camp, and I kept out of the R.S.M.'s way as much as I humanly could. When he came near me on parade, I was pulling faces. I was only a youngster, and he frightened me, that man.

My next posting was to Marchwood, Southampton, on a rigging course, and I duly arrived there, after a night at Liss, where I was mistakenly sent to begin with.

Marchwood was a beautiful little spot, and I enjoyed being there. We were the other side of the docks, and we could see the majestic bulk of the *Queen Mary* and the *Queen Elizabeth*, at anchor. Alas, there was the usual drawback – no football, and I still missed it, even though it was now early summer. Nor was the rigging course at the docks much fun.

I may not have been the Galileo of painting and rigging, but I think I knew my job, or presumably I wouldn't have been able to hold it. Down at Swansea, we would look at an object and say, "It weighs two tons." Much more often than not, we would be near the mark. But there, we had to work out a complex series of strains and stresses, and I found it a strain – on me. Fortunately I did not have to put up with it long.

From boyhood, I had been troubled with a recurring complaint, which might have exempted me from service, if I had not played it down. Today, happily, I am no longer troubled with it, but there had been a recurrence at Marchwood. None the less, it was a great surprise to me when I was ordered to the company office, and given a clearance chit. "Get your kit bag and pack up," I was told, nor did I have to hear it repeated. I was out. I was free. I could play football.

Not even my mother knew that I was coming home. I arrived on a Saturday evening, and she did not know whether to laugh or cry. I want back to my old job at Swansea Vale Smelter Works, and to my old place in goal for Winch Wen.

3
"ARE YOU A GOALKEEPER?"

Keeping goal for Winch Wen was a pretty busy job in those days. To be brutally honest, we weren't good. We were struggling, even in as uncelebrated a competition as the Swansea and District League. And although I was, in the vernacular, "glad of the work", the sequel when I returned to my real work on Monday mornings was not so pleasant.

One of my mates fancied himself as a humorist, and he found plenty of scope for his supposed talents in the many goals which I conceded, week by week. The climax came after a cup match against our nearest rivals, Samlet Stars, the team from Llansamlet, the next village. They were certainly stars compared with us, and we knew we were probably in for a hiding. We duly received it, going down by 7-1.

They made it a black enough weekend for me, in all conscience, and I was in no mood at all to be jeered at when I reported for painting and rigging, on Monday. But sure enough, my "humorist" was waiting for me, full of glee at what has so far, touch wood, been the highest score against me in my life.

I put up with it for most of the morning, until at lunch he said, "You wouldn't be in the side at all if it wasn't that your father was chairman." This was too much, and I wanted to go across the table and poke him one. Fortunately my other workmates held me back, and our difference was limited to a few hot words. It was not entirely smoothed over, however, for my tormentor took a piece of chalk and went around the factory drawing pictures of goal-posts in which a goalkeeper was diving one way, while seven footballs were going in the other.

The season 1948-49 wore on, with Winch Wen still struggling, until it came to the last match of the season, against Ivorites. Fate could scarcely have been more unkind to us, for it seemed that our biggest beating of all was reserved for the final game. Ivorites were really good, as good as we were bad. Indeed, they had already won the league. If we got away with an 8-0 beating, we reckoned that we would have done very well.

My mother, however, appealed to me to give the game a miss, so that I could attend my cousin's birthday party. "Don't play," she appealed. "Don't disturb the family harmony; after all, it's only the last match." Mother was entitled to make the demand, for she had always been a good friend to Winch Wen, laundering the team's kit and helping in dozens of different ways.

But I wanted to play. "I must," I told her; I felt that I couldn't desert Winch Wen when their backs were so hard against the wall.

So I failed to turn up on time for my cousin's "twenty-first" and turned out against Ivorites, instead.

By one of those weird and decisive ironies, it turned out to be one of the best games I had ever played in my life. Making a save or two early on, I found maximum confidence, reached form which I don't think I had ever quite shown up to then – and kept the Ivorites' forwards out. Twice, penalties were awarded against us, and each time I flung myself at the ball and managed to save.

The second penalty was taken by their left-half, Les Morris, a clever, canny player who had been an Arsenal junior at Margate, their pre-war nursery – but I got to that one, too. Meanwhile our forwards did their part and scored a goal, so that the result was a 1-0 win for us. The incredible had happened.

As I came off the field I was feeling pretty happy. We'd beaten the champions, another season was over – and now I was off to enjoy my cousin's party. Then I heard football boots thundering over the turf, behind me, and, turning round, I saw Les Morris and the referee haring in my direction as though someone were chasing them with a flame-thrower.

They reached me almost simultaneously, and the referee gasped, "How would you like to go to Bolton?"

"Yes," I replied, sceptically, "that's fine, but I've heard it before. I've had feelers from Swansea, feelers from Leeds, and nothing has ever come of it. I'm not interested any more." Which, I suppose, would be described as a defence reaction, because I was very interested indeed in turning my football-craziness into a way of earning a living.

Thus when Les Morris chipped in, "I've connections at Arsenal. If I wrote in, I could probably get you a trial," my first reaction, it's just words, was instantly followed by the afterthought, it's certainly worth talking about.

In the dressing-room, where both teams changed together, Les Morris kept pestering me, telling me how well he thought I'd played, how capably I'd taken the crosses. "Why doesn't he leave me alone?" I thought, resentfully. When I had changed I left the ground, hoping I would be left in peace. But as I strolled to catch my bus, there was the familiar thunder of feet behind me, and I didn't even need to turn round to know that it was Morris and the referee.

As we got on the bus, there was a hectic scramble between Morris and the referee to sit next to me, and I began to feel like some local belle at a party. Eventually Les Morris won, and in the five minutes which was all that bus ride to my house required, he talked like half a dozen radio commentators rolled into one. He got my height, my age and my weight, and he announced that he would "send these off to Highbury".

I didn't think too much about it, partly because it all seemed much too good to be true, and partly because I did not want to lay myself open to disappointment.

But the following Wednesday, round came Les Morris, triumphantly brandishing a letter. Jack Crayston, then the Gunner's assistant manager, had written to say that they were interested, and would like me to be fixed up in a top class Welsh league match, so that I might be watched. With the help of Les Morris, whose confidence I was far from sharing, I drafted a letter to the Llanelli club, asking for a trial with them.

They replied offering me a place in their private trial, and telling me to bring my own boots. I duly appeared, took my place in the trialists' eleven, and had the mortification of seeing my team do most of the attacking, so that I had little chance to show any form. There are times when a goalkeeper resents not being busy!

"That's that," I thought, when I made my way home. Nobody had said a word to me after the match as I was changing in the dressing-room. But once again, I had been too pessimistic. During the week I had a card from Llanelli to ask me to play in their reserve side, in the public trial. That not only meant I must have satisfied them, but assured me of having plenty of work to do, against their first-team forwards. It was my own fault, now, if I failed.

My anticipation was justified; I had plenty to do, and apparently I did fairly well. After the match, Jock Goldsborough, the Llanelli manager called me into his office. "Don't sign anything!" hissed Les Morris. "I'll be waiting outside in the corridor, and if you're asked to agree to anything definite, tell him I'm your brother and you'll have to consult me!" I promised I would.

The first thing Jack Goldsborough said was, "I like the way you performed. Would you like to sign on as an amateur?"

Warily I replied, "I'll have to ask my brother first," and when Jack Goldsborough asked where he was, I said, "Waiting outside." So Les was brought in, to say gravely that he did not think I was quite ready, yet; that I needed a few more games first, for Winch Wen.

When we were outside, he told me a little sadly, "I didn't see anyone there from Highbury. Perhaps they haven't bothered."

But again, the mid-week brought a letter. Highbury, apparently *had* bothered. The letter said that they had received a favourable report, and they wanted me to report to London for a further trial. Apparently we had been involved in a game of double bluff, for Jack Goldsborough had been detailed by the Arsenal to send them a report.

I need hardly say how excited I was. The world of football was opening for me, and though it wasn't Huddersfield Town to whom I might be going – the club I had dreamed of – it was instead a club if which I would scarcely have dared to dream.

Les Morris, bless him, accompanied me to London. He had been coaching me all through the summer on the Ivorites' ground, making me take the ball in the air, pull it down, kick it. Certainly he had helped me to improve.

I was due to keep goal at Highbury for a team of trialists against Chase of Chertsey, which was then the Arsenal nursery, producing such players as Brian Walsh and Brian Jackson. London was nothing new to me, as I had relatives in Plaistow, but the Arsenal Stadium nearly bowled me over when I had my first sight of it. Swansea Town's Vetch Field had been paradise enough for me, down in South Wales, and Highbury impressed me, as it soared above the streets of shabby houses, like a football Buckingham Palace. And the dressing rooms! There were baths, there were tiled floors; I had never seen anything like it. Certainly it was a bit of a change from the makeshift dressing-rooms in which I had been accustomed to strip.

The game, played before rolling, white empty terraces, was anti-climax. There was little for me to do, but just the same I let through a couple of goals, so that the result was a 2-2 draw. "That's that," I thought, as pessimistically as ever. Worse, I bent my thumb back painfully in making a save.

Playing in front of me was a cheerful young centre-half with dark, curly hair who seemed to represent the very essence of Cockney London. "How's your thumb, mate?" he asked me, after the match, so which I moodily replied, "All right."

The young centre-half thought, as he told me later, that I was a "miserable so-and-so". He was Len Wills, soon to become one of my greatest friends.

Despite my pessimism, however, Tom Whittaker called me up to his office, and there, behind the desk, I had my first sight of this burly, shirt-sleeved, middle-aged man, who was going to mean so much to my football career. Already I had met his elegant assistant, Jack Crayston, in circumstances that Jack will not readily forget. Les Morris had impressed on me, among a host of other things, the importance of a good firm handshake, and I had wrung Jack's hand as though it were a pump handle! "Like an octopus," he says, whenever I remind him of it.

In Whittaker's office I sat mute, admiring the multi-coloured banners which the Gunner's had brought back with them from tours all over the world, thinking how pleasant, and how unlikely, it would be, were I ever to participate in some of them. I did little or no talking; Les Morris, like a good Welshman, did that. "I'm not trying to sell you this boy," he said, having that very thing in mind, "but he is going to be great."

"All right," said Whittaker, at last, as I waited, breathless. "We'll sign him pro, or he can go back, if he likes, and play three months for Llanelli."

Oh, no, I thought; I'm not going to let a chance like this go by. "I'll sign," I said, and I did. I may add in parenthesis than since then Les Morris, then a railway policeman, now a detective, has found several likely young players in South Wales for the Arsenal.

Already I knew that I was going to be happy at Highbury. How could anybody doubt it after meeting Tom, after having his kindly greeting? I am not the first Arsenal player to say that he was a father to us; you could go to him at any time you liked, with any kind of trouble. At that time, he was, bar Haydn Green of Swansea, the only manager I had ever heard of. When he died so unexpectedly, it was a dreadful blow to all of us, and I realized how the Arsenal players of a different generation must have felt about the tragic death of Herbert Chapman.

Up to then, I had only once in my life even seen a match in London, and that was an amateur cup final, during my army days. I came up on an organized trip which included Ron Phoenix, later to become a Manchester City professional and, strangely enough, to make his league debut at Highbury. My army experiences being what they were, you will not be surprised to learn that I was in trouble on this occasion as well – in a typical army way. I went innocently enough into Lyons Corner House, put my hand into my pocket to take out some money, and was instantly picked up by a couple of superlatively efficient military police. They took me down the Marble Arch underground to ask me for my paybook, which, inevitably, I hadn't got, and then discovered that I had somehow come out without a pass, either. All I could show them was my National Service card, but the odd thing was that there was no sequel. I never heard another word.

I got back to Winch Wen in the early hours of the morning. What with Les Morris weaving plans for my future, it had been a remarkably swift train journey, but most of my excitement had evaporated by now. Thus it was with some calm that I was able to tell my parents that I had signed for the Arsenal. Naturally enough, they were delighted.

I had almost as much pleasure, next morning, in breaking the news to my tormentor, at work. But he took it exceedingly well, and had the kindness to wish me luck. My one fear was that there might be trouble in leaving my job and indeed, when I first gave my notice, the management wanted to know the reason, and said ominously that they didn't know whether they would be able to release me.

When I told them why I wanted to go, however, their attitude changed completely. "Certainly!" they said, and added, "you deserve the chance," though I doubt whether they even knew I was a goalkeeper, let alone whether they'd seen me play.

In any case, it was arranged that I should live in Plaistow, East London, with the family of my cousin, Tom Halley, who was employed at Austin Reed, the Regent Street outfitter. This meant that I would be encouragingly among known faces, right from the beginning. My great fear was that when I arrived at Paddington Station, Cousin Tom and I wouldn't recognize one another. When, a week after the news from Highbury – on a Sunday, to be precise – I travelled up from Wales, it was with many misgivings. I had told Tom to be beside the letter-box, at the end of the station. Would he duly be standing there?

Fortunately, he was; it was a happy ending to a journey which seemed to drag on for years.

The following morning, at ten o'clock, I reported at the Arsenal Stadium, and I don't suppose any young professional could have got off more solidly on the wrong foot. My experience was one of those which the Americans would have called "traumatic". Certainly I'm glad that I am a pretty elastic sort of fellow, temperamentally, or it might have taken a lot of getting over.

This is what happened. I saw Len Taylor, the cheerful and burly commissionaire, who immediately went to inform Jack Crayston of my arrival. I duly sat down in the foyer to wait...and wait...and wait. An hour passed. Two. Three.

"Maybe they've forgotten you," said Len Taylor, not without some reason. Maybe they have, I thought. I spent those wretched, weary hours staring at the bust of Herbert Chapman which ornaments the vestibule. I may not be an art critic, but there isn't a person alive who knows the details of that bronze better than I do, including its actual sculptor.

At three o'clock, Len Taylor ventured, "Have you had anything to eat?"

I had not. Len suggested that I trot down to the end of the road, where there was a cafe, and have a little refreshment. But, scared youth that I was, my one awful thought was that while I was eating, Jack Crayston would send for me – and he'd find that I was not there. But eventually Len promised that he would see to it that I was told, if anything of the sort occurred, and I went off to eat one of the most miserable bolted meals of my life. This is a fine club, I thought to myself, between one choking mouthful and another. I was to find out that it is indeed a fine club, but since I was eventually called into Mr. Crayston's office at five o'clock in the afternoon, my pessimism surely had some foundation.

After I had signed on, Jack Crayston introduced me to a stalwart, bald, middle-aged man. "This is George Male," he said, "he will be looking after you," and another famous name was fitted by a famous face. I knew all about George, of course, hero of so many England and Arsenal teams in the great pre-war days.

I was then told that I would be training under George, with the rest of the potential "A" team players, at the ground of the London amateur club Hendon, members of the Athenian League. It was a bit of a disappointment not to be training at palatial Highbury, which had made such a deep impression upon me, but I was not in any particular hurry. Les Morris, in fact, had said to me, "You will be in the Arsenal first team inside four years," and his prophecy was curiously accurate. For although I managed to play for the league team after less than two years, it wasn't until 1953 that I managed to become the regular keeper. There's something of the Druid about Les, perhaps...

George Male explained patiently to me how I could get to Claremeont Road, Golders Green, where the Hendon ground was situated, from Plaistow, but somehow or other, it just refused to sink in. I have the twin excuses, first that I was still in a pretty depressed condition, and second, that Golders Green, after all, is a very long way from Plaistow. At length, George kindly agreed to meet me on the platform at King's Cross, after I had cried hopelessly, "I'll never get there!"

We duly met, and travelled the rest of the way together. But when I had stripped and come out on to the pitch for training, I found there was another unpleasant shock in store for me. It appeared that Arsenal did not introduce people – a habit about which I shall have something more to say, later. When I got on top the field, all the boys had just finished doing their laps. "There you go!" said George Male. Did I? I thought. But with a mental shrug of the shoulders, and feeling extremely foolish, I began loping around the track on my own. How many laps should I do? I wondered. It was my first experience of this, the solid, traditional bedrock of British training, the grind that has made the British footballer what he is today. Anyhow, I compromised on six, by which time the rest of the boys were busily doing P.T.

Once again, I played my embarrassing game of O'Grady Says, fell in behind them, and imitated what they were doing to the best of my powers. After a while, a number of footballs were thrown out. A tall young man with fair hair, whom I afterwards found out was George Dunkley, went into goal at one end, and the other players began shooting at him. Nervously, I approached George Dunkley and whispered, "Would you mind if I joined you in goal?"

"What," he said, "ARE YOU A GOALKEEPER?"

It wasn't exactly a dream start but, in fact, I was to find out in due course that I had joined the finest club in football. I could not have made a luckier or happier choice. Arsenal for me, every time. I should add that after the training bout, I was presented to the rest of the lads, and began to find my feet.

All that first season, I trained at Hendon. Looking back, I do not regard it as one of the phases of my soccer career in which I made any great strides. What really good coaching there was came to a remarkable extent from Alex James, another legendary name for me. What a great little man he was, and how we all mourned his passing. In my boyhood, any paper that I picked up seemed to have the name of Alex James splashed across it, and I only wish I could have seen him on the field; those shuffling footsteps, long shorts and fantastically accurate passes which I've heard and read so much about. He was a blunt man, and never hesitated to tell you just where he thought you were going wrong (usually, I may add, with the utmost accuracy, too). He helped me quite a bit at Hendon, and later on he was to do an awful lot of good to big Jim

Fotheringham, our long centre-half-back. Only once did I ever step on to the same field in the same team as Alex, and that was in a charity match down at Horsham. Of course, it would be absurd to say that all the old skill and all the old mannerisms were there, but nevertheless, there were moments which recalled the genius he must have showed in the twenties and thirties. He was Mr. Blunt personified. Whether it was a friend or an enemy who happened to be involved, if there was anything he thought should be said, then Alex said it.

The first match I played was against March Town, at March, and apart from the fact that we managed to win it 3-1, there isn't much I remember about it. The third eleven, or "A" team, were playing all their matches of competitive standard in the Eastern Counties League, and its subsidiary cup competitions. My debut in that tournament was at Colchester, against Colchester United – the club from which Ted Platt had originally come. With all deference to Ted, I got sick of the sight of Colchester, for our away matches (they were practically all away) meant passing through Colchester. I detested that trip, and I came to know the dreary road (East Anglia, after all, is pretty flat, topographically) like the back of my hand.

Indeed, I haven't many memories of this rather dull league. At Gotleston, playing against shuffling Sailor Brown was rather a thrill. The former Charlton and England player, managing the local side, put in a couple of cracking shots, which made me think, "Oh ho, he's not finished yet."

But so far as the glamour that is Arsenal was concerned, all the contact we third teamers had with it was on Friday mornings, when we turned up to get our pay. Now and again, when for some reason we were not playing on a Saturday, we were able to go up there to watch the first team in action – and dream.

Naturally, I came to admire George Swindin, then keeping goal for the Arsenal. I am really not at all surprised that Tom Whittaker, in his posthumous autobiography, should have picked daring George as the finest goalkeeper he had ever seen at Highbury. I liked the way he came out to narrow the angle. He watched the ball intently and constantly, and until he injured a knee, he was always very agile. Perhaps his dives out of goal at the feet of opposing forwards were his strongest point of all. George was not, in my sense of the word, a spectacular goalkeeper. There was nothing show-offish about him. He always looked as safe as a rock, despite his acrobatics. Certainly he had none of the qualities of so many continental goalkeepers, who kick their legs into the air and throw themselves all over the goal for shots which I could catch between my teeth.

My first thrill came when, out of the blue, I was chosen for the reserves – and of all matches, for the one away to Cardiff City. This, to my immense delight, meant that my parents would be able to come across and see me play. I had been to Ninian Park to see a few matches, including Welsh internationals, though of course this was going to be a pretty pale affair by comparison with those occasions which provide an excuse for fifty thousand Welshmen to tie leeks on the goalposts and go stark, shouting mad.

In our side that day was no less a sporting figure than Denis Compton, playing on the left wing. Among the other members of the side were Arthur Milton and Alex Horsfield, who scored a bumper crop of goals in the Football Combination, without ever getting a match in the league team at Arsenal. It was beyond the midway mark of the season, and the reserves had been putting up a pretty good show in their league. I hoped I would not let them down.

Luckily, I was able to make a particularly good start, the Cardiff forwards keeping me busy in the opening minutes. Eventually, we won by the only goal. I remember an incident late in the match, when Cardiff Reserves were battling away for the equalizer. I came out to catch a high ball, and Tommy Best, the coloured centre-forward, came running in and hit me slap in the midriff, with his not inconsiderable weight. I went flat on the ground, the ball ran loose, and Tommy, who hadn't heard the referee's whistle blow for a foul, went charging delightedly away up the middle, eager for the congratulations of his team mates. Then, poor chap – anti-climax, as he realised that the ball was being placed for a foul. Bert Owen, our second team trainer, came on to give me attention, while the crowd gave the referee the bird. Those fellows can never do right, can they?

At the end of the game, which came soon afterwards, I had just trotted into the back of the net to retrieve my cap when a man in the stand shouted out, "You yellow b____." This annoyed me a great deal, for my parents were sitting quite near him, and I gave him a contemptuous sign. But I was to find out that this sort of thing did not pass muster at Highbury, even when it came out under provocation. I was hauled on to the mat the following Monday, and told off.

The following season, a reserve match at Cardiff, in which I figured once more, produced a rather strange sequel. At half-time, we Arsenal players came on to the field sniffing ammonia capsules, which we dropped just before we came on to the pitch. A miserable local reporter, thinking he'd come upon something very special – and his illusion was supported by the fact that fumes were given off in the cold – accused us of having smoked in the dressing-room! When the truth of the matter was made clear, the club naturally received an apology.

This was 1950, the year in which Arsenal embarked on their remarkable cup run, which ended happily at Wembley without entailing a single match outside North London. Sheffield Wednesday, Swansea Town, Burnley and Leeds United were all accounted for at Highbury. Next came the semi-finals against Chelsea, those two historic games, staged at the Gunner's war-time home of White Hart Lane, Tottenham.

I was well and truly one of the Arsenal family by this time, feeling and thinking with the league – and cup – team. So you can imagine how depressed I became when a couple of brilliant first-half goals from fair-headed Roy Bentley had Arsenal rocking on their heels. I could see those Wembley domes hovering somewhere in front of me like a mirage, only they were hovering there for Chelsea, and not for us. For us, in fact, the bell appeared well and truly to have tolled. Chelsea are there, I thought, miserably. We can't get two goals back.

But I had reckoned without the famous Arsenal spirit, and a touch of what unkind people are inclined to call our luck. On this particular occasion, perhaps they had some basis for their cynicism, for Freddie Cox's corner-kick (he still swears that he produced it by design) swerved and jinked in the wind like a football possessed, swirling at last past poor Harry Medhurst, into the top near corner of Chelsea's net. I flung my gloves high into the air in my uncontrollable delight, and I never saw them again. I didn't care about that. Big Leslie Compton's header, when he disobeyed Mercer's orders and trotted up to meet a corner from his brother, Denis, made the scores level after half-time, and we won the replay. But in retrospect, I do feel sorry for Harry Medhurst. I should hate to have anything as unpleasant as that happening to me; though Peter McParland's goal on the occasion of my first international runs it pretty close. More of that, however, in its place.

I was, by now, one of the biggest fans the Arsenal had, inside or outside Highbury, and everything they did was right for me. Not to be able to see the Cup Final was rather a blow. Instead, I turned out in the reserves away to Crystal Palace. For some reason or other, reports came through that both goals against Liverpool were the work of "Pete" Goring, who was leading the attack. We were all delighted, since we considered young Peter very much one of us. It was therefore a slight disappointment to learn that the goals had been thumped home not by Peter at all, but by Reg Lewis. Still, the Gunners had won the cup, and that in itself was enough to send us whooping with delight in the dressing-room; even if we had not been at Wembley to witness the victory.

The semi-final apart, the only cup match I managed to see on the way to Wembley was that against Leeds United, in the sixth round – at Highbury, of course. Reg Lewis's goal won that match, too, but the game was a drab and dreary one. It was my first sight of that notable young giant, John Charles, who was then United's eighteen-year-old centre-half. I cannot remember being much impressed, on that first occasion, by anything but John's exceptional size, though I was destined to revise my opinion in due course. I recall that he took a nasty tumble into the "moat" around the pitch, beneath the crowd on the terraces; the consequence of a splendid spurt to prevent the ball going behind for an Arsenal corner. I also remember how repelled I was by the Leeds colours of yellow and blue!

The season over, I went back to Wales for a pleasant holiday, with plenty of cricket on the beach. I had managed to get into the reserve team in my first season, and the club had won the Cup. I was pretty happy.

4
ARSENAL'S TELEPHONE JOKERS

The following season, 1950-51, I began training, to my great delight, at Highbury. Jack Crayston called me aside in the summer training days to say, "You look like being a regular in the reserves this season, but you've got to aim higher than that." It sounded encouraging.

One's first Highbury "ordeal" was to be thrown bodily into the cold plunge bath, an initiation which lies in store for every newcomer. This chilling experience over, I gradually began to fall in with the scheme of things, though training with the older lads was a bit strange to me, at first.

It was nice to find a fellow South Welshman there, in Ray Daniel, already well and truly launched as a bright young centre-half, and due to play against England at Sunderland that November, although he was still in the Arsenal Reserves. That day, by an odd coincidence, Big Leslie Compton was the England centre-half. "At least," I thought, teaming up with Ray, "there is someone whom I can talk to."

At Hendon, my chief companion had been a sturdy little Scottish inside-left called Charlie Carson, who had been signed almost on the very same day as me. This led to a rather odd confusion, the souvenir of which has tracked me down the years. Charlie, you see, had previously been a blacksmith, and somehow or other, the label got tagged on to myself. When Charlie left Highbury – he was one of those highly promising players who somehow did not quite "train on" – the tag still stuck. Charlie was always very quiet, and when he did say something it was rather hard to understand him, such was the density of his Scottish accent.

I received a lot of support and first-class advice during this period from Alf Fields, the club coach and former centre-half, who lived quite near to Plaistow. We would travel to Highbury together each day, and the tall, quiet, kindly Alf would pack those journeys with wise counsel. He had been associated with Arsenal since 1936, and had been playing such wonderful football at the start of the 1947-48 championship season that it looked as though Leslie Compton, who was still cricketing for Middlesex, might even fail to win back his place.

But in the sixth match of Arsenal's explosive beginning – they won all six – Alf sustained a knee injury in a home game with Bolton Wanderers, and the poor chap never played again for the First Division side. He did turn out for the "A" team, and on one occasion was the cause of an appreciative letter being sent to the Arsenal by Fulham. Alf had been skippering a side of youngsters at Craven Cottage, and giving them of good advice in the course of the game. But such was his impartial zeal for the game itself that he forgot his allegiance, and began coaching the Fulham lads as well! One fact about Alf which is not generally known – he never mentions it – is that during the war, he won the British Empire Medal with the Army in Italy. Now, he is fittingly in charge of coaching at Highbury. I readily set on record here the debt I owe him for his help in these vital early seasons.

Generally speaking, training at Highbury at this period was a good deal less exhausting than I had been given to expect. It's pretty tight now, but in those days, there was a little clique of players most of whose time was spent, somewhat compulsively, on the head tennis court, by the ground. This they occasionally alternated with a snatched cigarette in the treatment room. Once, when I lit up in there myself, while waiting for a friend, I was promptly booted out. I thought this was a little unfair. As in the wide world outside, there appeared to be one law for the rich and another for the poor.

The two great comedians at Highbury were Ted Platt and a tall, humorous East Londoner, Arthur Shaw, a wing-half-back who turned out many a time for the first team, without ever quite winning a regular place. But his morale value at Highbury was high. He and Ted would constantly and gravely be passing round notes inscribed, "Please ring Mr. C. Lyon, Primrose 3333." Sometimes, the recipient would do so, to find that this was the number of the London Zoo.

I remember a classic joke played on Jack Crayston, on the occasion of a reserve match at Bournemouth. We parked the coach on the promenade, and as we got out of it, the quick eye of Arthur Sharp noticed a telephone box and a tobacconist's shop, across the road from it. He took down the number surreptitiously, then strolled, carefully casual, up the road until he reached another phone box. From there, he dialled the number of the first, and of course, the bell began to ring.

"Quick, Jack," said Joe Wade – who was in the conspiracy – to Jack Crayston, "answer the telephone." Jack, public-spirited as ever, obeyed. A voice at the other end asked, "Would you mind doing me a great favour? Pop across to the newsagent opposite and tell Pegleg that Nobby won't be able to come tonight."

Jack said he would. He walked across the road, into the shop, and peered over the counter in search of a wooden leg. Nobody appeared to have one. Hopefully, he gave the message.

"There's no Pegleg here," said the newsagent. "You'd better try the shop up the road." Jack did. There was no Pegleg there, either.

He got back into the coach, counted up all the straight-faced boys, and drily remarked, "Yes, I'm Pegleg."

That was amusing, but it wasn't quite as cool as the telephonic joke which Arthur played on Ernie Collett, another former Arsenal player who became a trainer-coach. Ernie loves talking football, at any hour of the day or night, which led no doubt, to the rather unkind crack that he is the only man who ever talked his way into an Arsenal team, and played his way out!

Anyway, to appreciate this particular joke of Arthur's, you must know that there is a small office between the treatment-room and the dressing-room, which contains three telephones. Arthur calmly picked up one of them and rang the number of one of the others. Ernie Collett, who was in the room at the time, picked up the receiver, as he was intended to. Arthur was talking to Ernie, all the while, to screen what he was doing.

When Ernie answered the phone, Arthur demanded in a brusque voice, "Is Billy Milne (the trainer) there?"

"I'm afraid he isn't," said Ernie.

"Bert Owen, then?"

"I'm afraid he's not here, either."

"Where are they all?" Arthur snapped. "What's wrong with the place? Are they on strike, or something?"

"Who *is* that?" Ernie asked.

"This is Sir Bracewell Smith's (the chairman's) secretary. Who are you?"

"I'm Collett, sir," said Ernie respectfully.

"I want to know who you are, not what you've got. What are you?"

"I'm the "A" team trainer, sir," said poor, flustered Ernie.

"Then you're just the man I'm looking for. Get your bags packed, come over here, and give me a rub down."

"But there are two trainers missing, sir," Ernie protested.

"I'm Sir Bracewell's secretary," was the sharp reply. "Do as I say. Pack your bags and come over."

Ernie rang off in a terrible state of agitation, torn between his duties at Highbury, and his obvious fears of offending someone so close to the ear of the chairman. At length he was so perturbed by the dilemma that Arthur confessed the joke, which Ernie, I must say, took extremely well.

He's something of a humorist himself. "See this bald head," he sometimes says. "That's through taking George Swindin's goal kicks!"

This head tennis craze rather bewildered me. Some of the lads would play from ten to twelve, and if we were on the number one court, we were promptly turned off. Perhaps it was a good thing, for at least we got in some more varied training. One great training drawback for a goalkeeper, however, was that it was carried out on the hard practice pitch round the back of the stands. You couldn't go down for a ball, for fear of badly grazing your knees. We had quite a few five-a-side matches on it, which was a novelty from Hendon, but I wasn't happy at not being able to dive about, as goalkeepers should.

I had a pretty fortunate season in the reserve team, playing twenty-three games. We beat Chelsea 5-0 in the final of the league (the winners of the A and B sections used to play off) and won our way through to the final of the combination cup, in which we finished as runner-up to Charlton Athletic. I remember the match against Chelsea, when we tanned them at Stamford Bridge, their own ground, chiefly for the appalling conditions in which it was played. There was a blinding hailstorm, and such was the strength of the gale that a goal kick would never travel more than six yards beyond the edge of the penalty-area.

Ray Daniel, of course, was one of our chief stars, and a very able centre-half he was, quick, mobile and powerful. In those days, however, I found Ray a rather difficult centre-half to play behind. Now, I am more accustomed to doing so, but none the less, though Ray was my club colleague, I've always felt safer in Wales' matches, playing behind the rock-like John Charles. The trouble was I never quite knew what Ray was going to do next. Once, in a league game at Liverpool, he shaped to pass the ball back to me, and I promptly dived. But instead, he drew back his foot at the last moment, *then* passed back. I just managed to scramble the ball away, after a very nasty moment.

Arthur Milton was another of our stars, and he, too, was destined for international honours in the surprisingly near future. On our right wing, the fair-haired young Gloucestershire cricketer showed a tremendous burst of acceleration, which could take him hurtling past a back and on, towards the goal mouth. He had fine ball control, too, and every now and again goalkeepers would be reminded that he possessed a stinging shot. In practice matches, he was wont to go in goal, and he once played for half a match there, at Leyton, when George Swindin was injured.

At the beginning of the season, you could rely upon it that this quiet, dry, deliberate fellow would be talking about cricket. "I only needed six for the hundred, but then I played a silly shot." I am convinced that Arthur's early selection for England was the crisis point in his career. You may remember that in November 1951 Tom Finney dropped out of the game with Austria at Wembley, at a time when injury was knocking out the England players like flies. To the general astonishment, England sprung one of their now familiar Wembley gambles by picking Arthur, who had played no more than a dozen first team matches, and was having what was only his first full season in the league side.

Arthur failed to shine, and he never looked the same player after that, at least to my eyes. It seemed to be a terrible blow to his confidence, and I am convinced that undue haste lost England a dangerously effective winger. Indeed, it wasn't very long before he gave up soccer altogether, to give his attention to playing cricket for Gloucestershire.

This was the season in which Cliff Holton, hitherto a full-back, emerged as a hard hitting centre-forward. It was one of those strange combinations of events which produced a good new player. Arsenal Reserves were short, through injury, of a centre-forward, and Jack Crayston desperately telephoned Tom Whittaker, who was in charge of the first team, up at Blackpool. "Play Holton there," said Tom, with extreme foresight. Jack did, and Cliff was a tremendous success. He turned out against Reading, and all through the match, he was shooting away at goal from all angles. What shots they were, too! I rate Cliff as the hardest shot I have ever had to face. If ever he got a loose ball as a centre-forward, then – crack!

I still remember a goal I saw him score against Chelsea in a mid-week evening match. He must have been a good forty yards out when he steadied himself and let fly with that pulverizing right foot. The ball flew past poor, stunned Bill Robertson like a blazing meteor, landing in the top corner of the net. There's little that a keeper can do against that sort of bombardment.

Later, of course, Cliff became a wing-half, but I do not think it has ever been his best place. I myself think he would make a cracking centre-half. He has the power and the height, while he is the sort of player who would certainly try to use every ball. Cliff, besides, is a young man who is extremely sure of himself, though he isn't especially talkative; and self-confidence helps a great deal when your job is to seal up the middle.

John Chenhall, later to play regular Second Division football for Fulham, is another reserve colleague whom I well remember. John always impressed me as a swashbuckling type. A big, hefty, health-and-strength fellow, we used to call him "Garth", and he walked with an appropriate swagger. He is a Bristolian, like Arthur Milton – and, incidentally, like an Arsenal player more illustrious than either, Eddie Hapgood. It's strange how that pleasant West Country city produced soccer stars, as though by conveyor belt.

John did a bit of boxing as a youngster, and I believe it had affected his eyesight a little. At any rate, he would come up to the team sheet and squint at it with difficulty, as though he were searching hard for his name. He's a back, of course, and he was terribly unlucky not to win a championship medal with the First Division side in 1952-3. Poor John needed but a solitary game to clinch it, and Tom Whittaker promised he would slip him in, to see he received his deserts. But the fight grew hotter than anyone had anticipated, till the very last match of the season became decisive – and John never got the chance. Nothing worried this strapping fellow, who dressed brightly in tartan shirts. I remember once driving back with him from the West Country, where we had been playing a reserve match. Suddenly there was a colossal "Bang!" from behind as another vehicle ran into the back of us.

"Oops!" said John. "Good health!" And that was all.

Presiding benevolently over us all there was, of course, Tom Whittaker. "Don't call me Mr. Whittaker," he said to me, in my early Arsenal days, "or I shan't know who you're talking to. Call me "Boss" or call me "Tom"." After that, I always called him "Boss". "Tom", somehow, seemed a bit too familiar.

You could go to Tom with any problem, and he would always have time for you. He was a great kidder, too. You might tackle him with what you considered to be a hundred per cent concrete case, a grievance which he could not possibly talk you out of, and he would still contrive to show you that you were wrong. You'd come out thinking you were right, of course, but it did not alter the fact that Tom, yet again, had enjoyed the better of the argument.

I remember how I once tried, but failed, to kid him. I might have known it was hopeless. We players were issued with a couple of books of season tickets each season. A friend of one of my combination team colleagues wanted to go to a certain match against Blackpool, for which there was a tremendous demand. Since I had not promised my passes to anybody, I agreed that he should have one of mine. But he then, quite unforgivably, proceeded to sell it at a profit. Alas, the man who bought the ticket was sufficiently annoyed to send the counterfoils back to the club, and, of course, they were traced to me.

Tom sent for me, and confronted me with them. At first, I tried to convince him that I had lent the book to a friend. "Then he's let you down," said Tom. "He's sold them. Tell me straight – who got the tickets."

"I gave them to a friend," I insisted.

"Oh, no you didn't", said the Governor, and eventually the story came out. I had not wanted to implicate my friend, who, after all, had been let down badly himself. From that day, however, the system of issuing duplicate counterfoils for these season tickets was permanently scrapped.

Tom was tremendously strong. Sometimes we would lark about with him, to find, rather humiliatingly, that he could keep us under control with one finger, or a solitary thumb. Often we would threaten to throw him into the cold plunge, which would elicit the reply, "It would take ten of you to do it, and I'd probably take five of you with me!"

Jack Crayston was just as popular in his own way – and now that he is manager, Tom's successor, he's just as well liked and highly respected. He well deserves his nickname of "Gentleman Jack". Beautifully dressed, elegantly mannered, quietly spoken, with a wonderful, ironic turn of humour, he's certainly in harmony with soccer's most "fashionable" British club, if I may so describe it.

Jack's so kind that it is almost a fault. I have always found that he is afraid of hurting people, and that, especially in those reserve days, he'd rather cover up, when you make a bloomer, than give you the stick you probably deserved. My mother is one of his greatest admirers, and woe betide anyone who dares to breathe even the ghost of a word against him. She calls him, "The finest gentleman I've ever met." He has always put himself out to get tickets for her and my father, whenever Arsenal or the Arsenal Reserves were playing in South Wales, with me in goal.

One of the stories which Jack tells best concerns Ted Drake and an Arsenal-Huddersfield match before the war, at Leeds Road – the ground which had once been my most cherished dream. Apparently these matches were notable, above all, for the titanic clashes of two strong men come face to face – in the persons of Ted and Alf Young, the rugged, blond Town centre-half.

At half-time in one of these matches, Jack relates, Young came off the field with a cut over one eye, the other eye closed and an arm tucked into his side, all souvenirs of the solid shoulder charging to which he and Ted had been subjecting one another. Ted Drake sank into his place in the dressing-room and remarked, "Damn fine match, good hard game, but Alf Young isn't half using his elbows." To which someone replied, "If he's using his elbows, what are you using – a sledge-hammer?"

After my sad, bad beginning against Charlton and the terrible Jeppson, I was happy and relieved to be picked in goal against Manchester United. The match was also notable for being the debut of Cliff Holton, at centre-forward, and Ben Marden, on the left-wing. Ben was a thoroughly useful player, but he was not terribly lucky at Highbury. A very direct player, perhaps he was not over-endowed with ball control, but he could certainly move down that wing – or into the centre, for a crack at goal. I remember one reserve match against the Orient when he must have touched the ball four times during the first half, and he scored three goals. After the game, George Male arraigned him, "What happened, Ben? You should have had four!" He's the only player I have ever known to be rebuked, after scoring a hat-trick!

Arsenal hadn't won away to Manchester United since before the war, so this Maine Road game looked just about as difficult as the Charlton match had appeared (and I stress that word) easy.

Our rather experimental team did not make a brilliant start, for by half-time the powerful United team had us three goals down. One of them was beautifully scored by the England international full-back, Johnny Aston, who was at that time leading the United attack. He beat Leslie Compton, and left himself with a clear path down the middle. I came out to meet him, and I'm pretty sure that I was so placed that I would have saved a shot. Johnny, however, did not give me the chance. He lobbed the ball perfectly over my head, and though I blundered back desperately, the best I could do was to finish in company with it – in the net. What a great start, I thought miserably. Eight goals in a match and a half – and there are three-quarters of an hour of this one to come.

As it happened, pessimism was not justified. I was quite pleased with the way the second half went, for I had quite a bit of work, but did not let through another goal. Indeed, we managed to get another one ourselves, thus making the final score 3-1. I came off the field after the match side by side with Reg Allen, the man who came back from a prisoner-of-war camp to become the most expensive goalkeeper at that time, in soccer history. "Never mind, son," he said consolingly, "don't worry; you did well enough. They can't blame you for this lot."

That was certainly an admirable Manchester United side, with Henry Cockburn, Stan Pearson, stalwart Allenby Chilton, and, of course, the peerless Johnny Carey. I always admired Johnny. That bald head seemed to stand out in every match.

Mind you, I had infinite admiration for our own driving skipper, Joe Mercer. From his position at deep left-half, Joe used to spur the side on – and on. He lived up in Cheshire, but would train with us now and again, on a Friday, and he was always very good to the younger boys. Certainly he was a good skipper, and you could approach him with any kind of problem. If he thought the Governor's decision or advice was needed, he would have no hesitation in trotting upstairs to sort it out for you. Not only would his fantastic energy keep Arsenal turning as though he were some footballing flywheel, but he would also exert quite a sway over referees. When they gave a decision against the Arsenal which he disapproved, he appeared to frighten them to such an extent that they'd often give us the benefit of the doubt on the next occasion. Sometimes I used to wonder how he got away with it, but he always did. By this time, of course, he was a bit of a football legend, which must have contributed.

I'll never forget his last game for us, against Liverpool, in May 1954, when he was carried off with a broken leg. When he was borne off on a stretcher, waving gallantly to the crowd, everyone in the stand stood up. They seemed to know that an era had somehow come to an end. As for me, I was standing in goal, and the tears were running out of my eyes.

After that Manchester United match, I was dropped, which did not really surprise me. Besides, it was tactfully done. "Well, leave you out for a few matches," Tom Whittaker told me, "so that you can get your confidence back. Eight goals in two matches are enough for anyone to take, for a time. I'm confident you'll be back."

So it was hallo again to the lukewarm bath of reserve team football, though not without a certain feeling of relief, mingled with my disappointment. But after a mere couple of matches, I was back again in the league side. It was a black Easter weekend. On Good Friday, we lost at home to Portsmouth, in what was a very good game. Duggy Reid, another of soccer's hardest shots, got the only goal of the game – though I should add in parentheses, he doesn't hit them as hard as Cliff Holton.

His slightly angled shot, with plenty of power behind it, was going away from me, and I dived. I managed to touch the ball with my finger-tips, but could not hold it. That was that; three games, and three defeats, two of them at Highbury.

The next day, a Saturday, victory came at long last. We defeated Wolves 2-1 at Highbury, and I was brought face to face with another of the hardest hitting forwards in the game, tiny Johnny Hancocks, the lightweight with the punch of a Marciano. I was relieved we'd won, certainly, but any satisfaction was diminished by the fact that I was injured.

It was a nasty injury too. As I rose to collect a high cross ball up went Royston Swinbourne, the Wolves centre-forward, and his knee accidentally drove hard into my back. It cost me a ruptured kidney, and to make matters worse, my parents were watching, though my mother is usually too nervous to watch me in first team matches. I wasn't carried off. I picked myself up and somehow managed to carry on, though I was in great pain, and I could not bend. I thought I must simply be badly bruised. At all events, I hung on, and there was the consolation of victory.

After the match, my father waited anxiously at the tea bar to hear what had happened to me. At last a message came to him, from me, that I would not be able to accompany him back to Romford, where he was staying with the Halleys. I was taken to the Royal Northern Hospital, and the club very generously put my parents up at Manor House. All being well, it did not seem that my ordeal would be a long one. Probably, it appeared, I would be hopping around again within about three days.

Alas, my luck was brutally out. On the third day I somehow or other succeeded in contracting chicken-pox. I was moved to the deserted top floor, and private nurses had to be brought in, so that they would not carry the germs. It never rains....

The time passed slowly, though Joe Wade kindly got a radio dealer friend of his to fix me up with a television. Thank goodness I had it, or I should have gone crazy with boredom, for naturally I was allowed no visitors. Those weeks cost Arsenal £140, but they paid it with typical good humour.

My distress was increased by the knowledge that the team was going to make its second post-war tour of Brazil, and that I must have stood a reasonable chance of being included on it. The doctor told me with emphasis that so long as there still were spots on my body, there was no question of any such thing. The next time I took a bath, I carefully rubbed all the spots out – but the doctor was not to be fooled so crudely. There was no tour for me, and it was as well, perhaps, that I did not go, for my body was not strong enough to resist further illness.

Somehow or other, it always seems to be Black Easter for me. In 1955, I was involved in a car crash. In 1954, I felt deaf and dizzy, and was forced to miss our home match – funnily enough, again against Portsmouth. But I turned out for the return at Fratton Park – unwisely, as it transpired. During the kick-in before the match began, I stooped to pick up a shot from Derek Tapscott, and went suddenly dizzy. All through the game, Len Wills had to shout to me when I needed to come out, and I somehow survived on ammonia sniffers. Now, I just dread it when Easter comes along.

Of the following season, I have little to say. The name of Kelsey passed into temporary and renewed obscurity, while George Swindin turned in the full forty-two league appearances. Arsenal got to the cup final again that season, and this time I was there to see them.

It was, if you remember, a team of crocks, and I thought it put up a very gallant fight against Newcastle United, after losing Walley Barnes with a badly strained knee, after twenty minutes. Ray Daniel had his wrist in plaster, Jimmy Logie had only just emerged from hospital, after a minor operation on his leg, and Cliff Holton, in for his first cup game at centre-forward, did not really come off that day, and never found his formidable shooting boots.

And yet, if that early, overhead shot by Duggy Lishman had only gone into the net instead of bouncing maddeningly on the bar, before sailing over, it might have been another story. Don't forget that the whole course of play would have been changed, for a start, so that the injury to Barnes would probably never have happened. But Newcastle won the cup and we, so they told us, won the glory – which did us a lot of good!

What *would* have happened if Duggy had scored? Probably Newcastle would have kicked off ....and scored four!

Almost like a Kangaroo. Leaping high for the ball in a match against Burnley at Highbury. The Burnley player is Leslie Shannon.

The five goalkeepers at Highbury when I first joined the Arsenal. *From left to right:* myself, Norman Uprichard, George Swindin, Ted Platt and George Dunkley.

The Winch Wen team. *Standing from left to right*: Hopkins, Leadbetter, Tucker, myself, Ford, Staddon; *kneeling*: Evans, Parvin, Rowden, Jones and Jenkins.

In action for Great Britain. I am seen about to clear in the match against the Rest of Europe at Belfast in August 1955. John Charles (No.5) had come to the rescue. Great Britain lost 4-1.

Head tennis during training at the Arsenal.

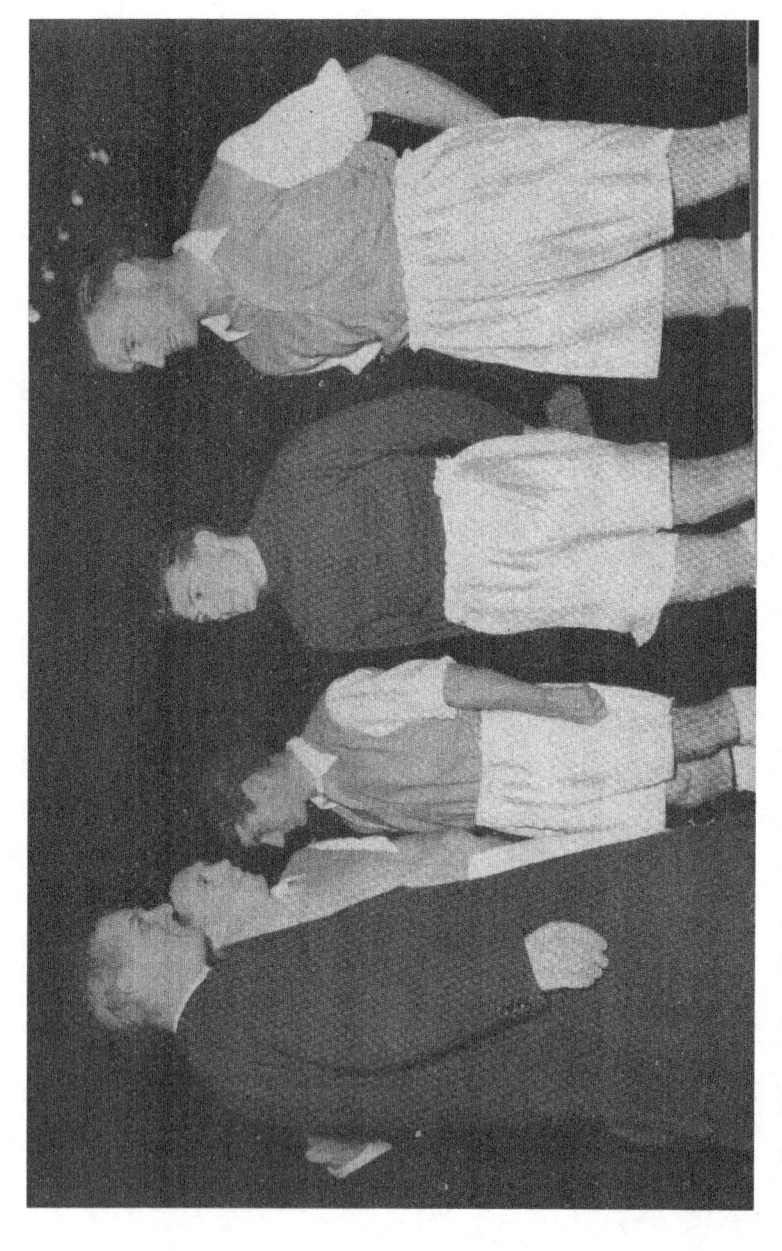

Joe Mercer introducing the Arsenal players to the Duke of Edinburgh before a match against Hibernian. I'm standing between Joe Wade and Lionel Smith.

Keeping fit in the Arsenal gymnasium at Highbury. The other players are Reg Lewis (left) and Jimmy Robertson (since transferred).

Putting a Perry (Blackpool) shot over the bar, at Bloomfield Road, as Brown rushes in. The Arsenal players in the picture are Roper, Dodgin and Wills.

5
LEAGUE CHAMPIONS

With season 1952-3, my luck at Highbury decisively turned. Not only did I win my way into the side as regular first team goalkeeper, but I was also fortunate enough to bag a league championship medal.

Yet I must admit I did not make a very brilliant start. I opened the season with five games in the reserves, then George Swindin dropped out of the first team with a wrist injury, and Ted Platt took his place. I wasn't playing too well and I knew it, but when the regular November trip to play Racing Club de Paris came round, and when I saw that my name wasn't even on the list as travelling reserve, I felt a bit hard done by. Ted Platt was between the posts, and George Swindin, his wrist still in plaster, was going along too – presumably for the ride. This, mark you, for a friendly match in which substitutes were permitted. What would happen if Ted got hurt? George wouldn't be able to do anything about it, while I would still be in London.

I therefore felt I had a grievance, and went to see Tom Whittaker about it. "I think this is a bit unfair," I told him. "I think it is my place to be going as reserve to Ted Platt. I know George Swindin has been a good club servant and all that, but after all, he isn't fit to play."

Tom's reply was pretty blunt. "You're just as likely to be dropped from the reserve side, the way you're playing at the moment." Out I went, my tail between my legs, thinking, I'm just as low as I can get, again.

But suddenly things started to break for me. That Monday, Ted Platt took part in a charity match, and suffered a bad knock. When the boys met at the Kensington Air Terminal, to take the coach out to the airport, he told Tom Whittaker that he did not think he would be able to play. Since there was no question at all of George Swindin taking his place, this put Tom right on the spot. Thus it was that when I arrived for training that morning at Highbury, Len Taylor, the commissionaire, told me, "Jack Crayston wants to see you."

I went. "Ted Platt has cried off the Paris trip," Jack told me, "and you must go instead. How long will it take you to go home, collect your stuff and get to the airport? You have to catch the one o'clock plane."

"I could manage it in three hours," I told him, "and that would be cutting it fine."

"Right," said Jack, "you'll have to do it faster." He hired a huge car, which purred creamily out to Romford with me – or at least, that was how it started. But the driver just had to pick that day to assert his originality, and try a new route through the East End. The traffic was chokingly heavy, and when we did at last get to Kensington, it was with only half an hour to spare. We met the men who were waiting there for me with the relevant tickets, telephoned the airport, and asked them to hold the plane. They agreed – but they said they would not hold it for an instant longer than five minutes. We just did it. I bolted through the customs, raced across the tarmac, got into the plane, the door slammed shut behind me, and we were off – on the first air trip of my life.

The only seat was right at the back, away from the rest of the boys, and I was a bit too scared to get up and move around. In fact, none of the party even knew I had managed to catch the plane at all, and Bob Wall, who was in command of the party, was surprised to see me get out, when we reached Paris.

I was very excited at visiting Paris, for it was my first trip abroad. It was very nearly my last, for as I came out of our hotel I looked the wrong way, and was almost run over. However, I survived to play that evening, in the floodlight game; and what floodlights they were. Certainly they ranked as the best I had seen until then, though the only others I had played under were our own, when we met Charlton in a reserve match. These Paris lights made the pitch as bright as though it was daylight, but at half-time, every light in the stadium suddenly went out, as though the electricity had been cut off at the main. It hadn't fortunately, and there were still some lights in the tunnel to the dressing-rooms, otherwise we might all have been playing blind-man's-buff in the dark.

We lost the match, 2-0, both goals going to their centre-forward, though the player I best remember was the coloured Moroccan half-back, Mahjoub. This French international (now that France and Morocco have gone their separate ways, he's no longer eligible) was in splendid form, popping up here, there and everywhere. He was a very strong tackler, a bit too strong at times, I thought, but he probably had more to do with one of his club's rare wins against us, than anybody else.

I was satisfied enough with the game I played; my form seemed to be coming back, and I had quite a few shots to save. There should, however, have been more; and thereby hangs the tale of my antipathy towards continental forward-lines. As a goalkeeper, I like plenty to do. The busier I am, the better I am pleased. In Great Britain, you know that in nine cases out of ten, when a forward is coming through, he will take a shot; but not on the Continent. They dally when it seems they ought to shoot, passing and repassing the ball. Then, as often as not, they shoot when you least expect them to.

Another feature which I didn't like was the behaviour of the crowd, which made me a bit nervous at times. Instead of the familiar English boo, they employed the piercing whistle to show their displeasure, and the way I took my goal kicks displeased them very much. They wanted, apparently, to see them taken in the continental way, by rolling the ball just outside the penalty-area to the full-back, who pushed it gently back into the goalkeeper's hands. Every time I took my run, the whistles rose to a hideous crescendo. I got used to it, however.

The following Friday, I was overjoyed to see my name on the team list. I had kept my place, and would be playing against Blackpool. It wasn't going to be an easy match. The seasiders had been scoring goals galore, and recently they had heavily defeated the Wolves. If I can keep them out, I thought, it will be more than even Bert Williams can do. The newspapers predicted that it would be "a trying time for Kelsey", even though the match was due to take place at Highbury.

We won, however, by three goals to one, even though the great Stanley Matthews was playing. I was surprised to find no difficulty in taking his centres. He floated them in very gently, and it was the easiest thing in the world to move out and pluck them out of the air. It was difficult when he came dribbling and swerving his way along the by-line, to drag the ball sharply back into the middle.

I kept my place for twenty-five matches. From a decent place in the top half of the table, we climbed steadily, until it became clear that we were in line for a tilt at the championship, then held by Manchester United. But United were in a transitional stage, and we knew we must have a chance. Over Christmas, we took five points out of six, and we entered the New Year brimful of confidence.

Meanwhile, I was trying to get back to my old form with crosses. Always, I had considered this one of my goalkeeping strengths, but the injury suffered against the Wolves had insidiously undermined my self-confidence, and I knew I was not performing as well as I should be. I had my own way of trying to practice my keeping, out on the hard practice ground, and in due course, I think I managed to remedy the trouble.

Getting a grasp of angles was also immensely important. One method I used was to line up five of the boys and get them to shoot at me. If I found myself within easy reach of the ball, I'd know that I had taken up the right position. If not, then I must change my ideas. I even got the ropes out, and this is a wrinkle which I can recommend to aspiring young goalkeepers.

You tie a long rope to each upright, then take each of them out in a straight line so that they converge on the point from which the imaginary shot is going to be made. You must then position yourself so that you are the same distance away from each rope. That means you are placed as well as you humanly can be, to deal with the shot.

That goal by Johnny Aston taught me something, too. Since then, I have always tried to trick the oncoming forward. I will come out of goal just so far; far enough to have a chance of blocking any shot that may be made, but not so far that I am left without a chance of recovery, if the forward should decide to try a lob.

Playing in professional football, I had had to curb my spirit of adventure. Back in the Winch Wen days, I had tended to consider that any ball in the penalty-area was mine, even if it happened to be floating across the eighteen-yard line itself. But one could not do that in First Division football, for fear of what would happen if one was challenged and dropped the ball. Now, I do not go a yard beyond the goalkeeper's area. I'm governor of the six-yard box, I like to think – but that's as far as it goes.

When the cup came round, I was able to make my debut in the competition against Doncaster Rovers, at Highbury, when we had an easy 4-0 win. Another Second Division Club, Bury, followed them to North London, and we disposed of them, 6-2. But then the luck of the draw left us, and we had to travel away to Burnley.

Winning at Turf Moor is always a very tough job, even though Arsenal have really done rather well there, since the war. Burnley had an excellent defence at that time, and there was not much wrong with their forwards. But we beat them, and I shall always remember the match as one of the finest Arthur Milton ever played. He scored both the goals in our 2-0 win, the second coming after a really wonderful individual run. The first was easier, for Jimmy Strong dropped a lob in the very goal mouth, and Arthur pounced on the gift.

Burnley gave us plenty of trouble, and red-haired Alex Forbes spent a good deal of time chasing Billy Elliott down the Burnley left-wing. They had cool, elegant Tommy Cummings at centre-half, grave Jimmy Adamson beside him at right-half, and the dangerous head of Bill Holden, in the middle of their attack. Bill got quite a few headers in, and I found myself twisting and turning to catch them, or push them over the bar. Others, which beat me, were fortunately just a little off the target, and finished outside.

Bill wasn't an especially hefty centre-forward, but he was, and remains, the sort of player who never gives a goalkeeper much peace. He was always challenging, so that you knew, when a cross came over, that if Burnley were the other side, it was never going to be just your ball. Bill was going to be somewhere with you, so that you had to think about the ball and him.

I may add, in parentheses, that I don't mind actually being challenged for the ball by shoulder-charging forwards. I've honestly never been able to see that it does them much good. Once I admit, I was upset by a player who kept coming at me, and largely thanks to my mistakes, we lost a match at Highbury. But the thing that upset me was chiefly what he was calling me. Perhaps I'm sensitive.... The odd thing is that the forward in question has always seemed to me a nice, quiet gentlemanly fellow, off the field, both before and since those unpleasant incidents. One of these days perhaps someone will make a study of the changes that take place in certain boxers when they duck under the ropes, and certain footballers when they step out of their dressing-rooms. It might produce some instructive and fascinating results.

We didn't win the cup that season, of course, for Blackpool put us out in the next (and sixth) round. Having dished them 3-1 in the league, we were fairly sure that we could manage it again, especially as their post-war record at Highbury had been pretty dim. But they really did play some good stuff, and their first goal, scored by their wee inside-right, Ernie Taylor, was a beauty. Ernie is another of those little footballers, in the Hancock's mould, who punches a great deal harder than his height and weight.

Stan Matthews made the running for the goal. Dribbling and swerving like a possessed eel, he drew practically all of our defence to one side, then crossed the ball for Ernie Taylor to run on to it at full-pelt. Crack! went Ernie, and the ball flashed past me, a foot inside the right-hand post. It was certainly a magnificent shot.

Arsenal, in typical fashion, however, hit back to equalize. Scottish international George Farm, Blackpool's clever, unorthodox keeper, was harassed by big Cliff Holton, as he went out to gather a high ball. George came down with a bump, there was a pile-up in the goal mouth, the ball ran loose, and, to the roaring delight of the crowd, little Jimmy Logie slipped it into the net, for one of his rare goals. We were level.

I thought to myself, we're in with a chance, even if it does mean going to Blackpool. Alas, I was rather premature. Almost in the next minute, Alan Brown came thundering after a long ball, pushed through our defence. I could see at once that my only chance was to come out – and come out as fast as I could. It was Alan or I, as the big Scottish international came thundering after the ball. I came towards him as though we were a couple of knights on horseback, jousting in a tournament. I thought it was my ball, but alas, I did not bargain for Alan's speed. He was there first, by a split second, shot just as I dived, and the ball passed under my body and into the net. No Wembley for us.

And none for Alan Brown either, poor fellow. His left shin met my hip at heaven knows how many miles an hour, and it stopped him dead. There was no crack, and Alan staggered on for another six yards or so, before collapsing. I did not realize that he had actually broken his leg, but thought he was just badly shaken up. "Don't move my leg," he gasped, as his trainer came on to the field, "I think it's broken." He was carried off on a stretcher, but, since I did not think he had been so badly injured, I was not as upset as I would otherwise have been. In fact, by one of those ironic tragedies of the game, Alan, the man who had helped to put Blackpool in the final, missed that match himself, for the second time in three years. He'd been forced to cry off in 1951, too.

Perhaps the leg has just gone numb, I thought, as I made my way off the field. But I was told that it had been X-rayed, and there was no doubt about it; it had been broken. I went in to see Alan lying on the table in the treatment room, and I felt rather sorry, in spite of our own disappointment. He's put them in the semi-final, I thought, and now he won't be there himself. Alan, like the good sport he is, had words of reassurance. "Don't worry," he said, "it was a pure accident. Something had to go."

I wanted to visit him in hospital, the following Monday, but by then they had already moved him off to Blackpool, and it wasn't possible. The next time we met was at Blackpool; at Bloomfield Road, in a match. Neither of us seemed to have learned our lesson, for we both went charging in for a cross – and finished together, in the back of the net. It can be hard, this game.

One match played that season which I shall always remember was a friendly under floodlights against Hibernian, early in the winter, played in aid of the Duke of Edinburgh's National Playing Fields Appeal. I rank it, indeed, as the greatest game I have ever played in, to date, and the Duke seemed to be of the same opinion, since he afterwards described it as "the greatest game of football I've ever seen". We were presented to him beforehand, and I think the match must have brought in a good deal of money to help his fund. He had quite a chat with Jimmy Logie, who had been in the Royal Navy during the war, about the sea, and perhaps that was what inspired this fine little Scottish footballer to play such a wonderful game.

They say that departed sons take a malign pleasure in reminding their home towns of what they have missed. Jimmy, of course, comes from Edinburgh, and that evening he tore the Edinburgh team's defence into ribbons, with all the wonderful close control and subtlety in passing that distinguished his game at its best. That night, he played himself belatedly into the Scottish team because their selectors, apparently, had been watching television. It was his only cap, which is a reflection of how little international honours can mean, when it comes to estimating the worth of a player. As far as I was concerned, Jimmy for years just *was* the Arsenal, the indispensable link between attack and defence.

Everybody seemed to play well that night, and five of the goals in our 7-1 win went to Don Roper, playing at centre-half. I believe Don started his career there as a youngster with

Southampton, during the war, and his father was a pro centre-forward; but of course it was as a winger that he made his name – or as a back!

I shall never forget seeing Don giving as perfect a full-back display against Stanley Matthews as I've ever witnessed. I was up in the stands that day. Leslie Compton was injured and went to the wing, Don played at back for the rest of the game, and Matthews scarcely had a smell of the ball, so fast, decisive and well judged were Don's interventions. But there are few backs who can do that sort of thing to Stanley twice. When Don tried it again, a year or two later, it just didn't work, and Stanley fooled him just as he has fooled so many defenders, before and since. That day I was playing, and had an ominously closer view of the Matthews wizardry, in a match which ended in a 4-4 draw.

In attack, Don was a good trier, always looking for goals, and he certainly had a powerful left foot.

A word or two on the Arsenal pattern of defence might be appropriate here, in this discussion of our 1952-3 championship side. It was and is based, of course, on the Pivot scheme, introduced by the late Herbert Chapman in the twenties. The centre-half, that is to say, stays in the middle, while the backs and wing-halves pivot on him. This is, to my mind, a far better system than having square-playing backs lying on top of the wingers; a scheme in which the inside-forward suddenly bursting through has an even chance with the covering-up full-back of getting the ball. Our backs will always hold off the tackle, knowing that they have done their job if the winger eventually crosses, for by that time the rest of the defence will have fallen back.

To give an example of how our defence works, let us say that the outside-left beats our right-back and cuts in on goal. Under the pivoting system, the Arsenal centre-half must come across to intercept, while his own place is taken by the left-back, who quickly moves into the middle. In turn, the left-half should be haring back to cover the left-back.

If the opposing centre-forward moves out to the wing, our centre-half must still remain in the middle. When the opposing leader does this, and their winger remains on the flank, thus giving them a "man over" with regard to our full-back, we are not greatly worried. They don't score goals from out on the wing.

Our backs in that championship season were Joe Wade and Lionel Smith, for Walley Barnes was still nursing his unfortunate cup final injury.

Joe had waited a very long time indeed for this chance, and he deserved better luck. It was good to think that he achieved a league medal and a Football League representative honour, to compensate him for all the patient years he'd spent in the reserves. His league debut, at left back (his more customary position) was made as long ago as 1946, and he was a regular member of the League South Arsenal team of 1945-6, often at left half.

I was always chummy with Joe, whom I regarded as another of football's gentlemen. A Londoner, dapper and dark haired, he had good manners, but a sense of humour which always seemed to be mixing him up in practical jokes and "phoney" telephone calls, in which he usually acted as the straight man.

As a back, this Hoxton man was good, sound and straight-forward. More than that, he was a man of ideas, an F.A. coach, and it was no surprise to any of us when he acquitted himself so well, afterwards, as manager of Hereford, in the Southern League. Even in his Highbury days, he was brimful of ideas, and during training would like to get us standing in a circle, each demonstrating a different exercise – or passing a couple of medicine balls around a human triangle.

Lionel Smith was an English international. Like Joe, he had spent quite a while in the reserves, though he'd been lucky enough to get into the team as a convert from centre-half to left-back, when Laurie Scott was injured, in 1948.

We called this tall, lean Mexborough Yorkshireman "Springfield", because we thought he looked like Gary Cooper, in the cowboy film of the same name. Lionel looks less like Gary Cooper, now that he, like Joe, is a manager in the Southern League, for he has put on a surprising amount of weight.

In my book, he was great for one thing above all, he never seemed to be beaten. A winger might pass him, then out would come that long left leg of his, and he would contrive to scoop the ball back. I remember how once we were watching a film which the Governor had had taken, of a match between us and the Spurs. The Spurs outside-right once swept past Lionel, to the accompaniment of friendly jeers from his colleagues in the "audience".

"Don't worry," said Lionel, "Smithy'll get him." And sure enough, the film shows Lionel chasing his man, out comes the old leg, the ball is scooped away and Smithy has cleared it up-field. Lionel was all left foot; the right foot was just to stand on, like my left! Once, after he had cleared off the goal-line in a Wembley match between England and Scotland, he remarked, "That's the best of having big feet."

I think we were a fairly good defence. I was so used to playing behind Joe Wade in the reserves that I found, reassuringly, that I seemed to know his every move. I knew, for example, that he would pass the ball back to me more often than Lionel, who was inclined to try and pull himself out of trouble.

At right-half there was Alex Forbes, the red-haired, tear-away Scot, the man who cannot travel by air, nor even, I suspect, on a bike. In aeroplanes, Alex was hopeless; there is just no other word. On the way back from Brazil once, on what was admittedly a rough and bumpy trip, he was sitting next to Reg Lewis in the aeroplane. "Oh, please God," he was muttering, "make this aeroplane crash, and put me out of my misery."

While Reg, beside him, was saying, "Please God, don't listen to him – I want to get home."

I liked playing behind Alex. Sometimes he was a bit venturesome, and he liked his little sorties up-field, which were inclined to leave us high and dry. But he was a very good player for all that, a strong tackler who wanted to use the ball. He liked to get it, too. When running alongside one of our own players who was in possession, he used to shout, in reminder, "Get your head up, son!" One trouble about his jaunts up the field is that the winger would move down the touch-line ahead of him, expecting the ball. Jim Logie would cruise along beside him, expecting the square pass inside – and Alex would just keep on keeping on, while shaping to give either pass. This meant that Jimmy, instead of dropping back to take his place, would be lured far up the field, and we were thus wide open to a counter-attack down the opposition left. Still, there is no question but that Jimmy and Alex worked very well together.

Jimmy was a shrewd mover of the ball, and pretty accurate. Through playing as far back as he did, he did not score many goals, but when he was in the penalty-box, he would snap up the occasional chance. He's a shrewd judge of a footballer, and knows when a lad is likely to make the grade. "He's going to be a good 'un," I sometimes would hear him say of a young player, and he was often right. Jimmy is a quiet little fellow, and you had to know him really well, before you could talk to him.

He made many a chance for big Duggy Lishman, at inside-left. Duggy was always direct, rather than a schemer, and I would define him, with every respect, as a "poacher". A poacher, not of rabbits, but of goals, his trespassing preserve the opposing penalty-area. Since there's hardly room for two scheming inside-men, in the same attack. Duggy liked to put "side" on his shots, sometimes, like an expert billiard player, and I've seen him score many a goal like this. He was also exceptionally dangerous with his head-flicks, and was expert in turning low crosses from Freddie Cox into the net; corners, too, for that matter. Off the field, Doug went his own way, and he was never a member of the head-tennis "clique". I found him rather reserved and fairly quiet. On the field, he was a great asset, and he could afford to be "The Poacher", as we called him, with a player like wee Jimmy in the side.

Alas, I was destined not to keep my place in the team till the last, vital, thrilling weeks of the season. I was dropped after the Easter Saturday match against Liverpool at Highbury, which we lost 5-3, but not without a number of frights. I was considered responsible, probably justly, for a couple of the goals, and since the race at the top of the table was getting so intense, it was decided to bring back George Swindin for the last seven games. Good enough, I thought, for if George does play in those seven games, he'll have reached the fourteen-match minimum which qualifies him for a championship medal; his third. I myself had already been in the side twenty-five times, so I was already well past the safety mark.

Tension mounted almost intolerably, until a mid-week match against Burnley, our last of the season, became vital. If we won it, we would pip Preston North End on goal average alone, and just nose our way home, ahead of the field.

Watching it from the stand, from the players' paddock, as we call it, was torture. I was sitting next to Freddie Cox, and I must have knocked lumps out of him, when we scored our three goals. I remember his protesting, "Cool down a bit, Jack!"

Joe Mercer, a captain courageous as ever, made the score 3-1 for us in a goal-mouth scramble (I nearly knocked Freddie out of the stand at that point!). Burnley hit back to make it 3-2, and the last agonizing minutes were the story of our defence resisting their nippy attack. Arsenal, rightly or wrongly, seemed to be concentrating on having what they held. The Governor could not stand any more of it, and went quietly and palely down to the dressing-rooms, for the last five minutes. They seemed like days, those closing stages, but we just held out. I rushed down at once to shake hands joyfully with everybody, then I sat down on one of the benches in the dressing-room and became a little sadly reflective.

I've played twenty-five matches, I thought, but it's these players who won tonight who will be the heroes. At that moment, something very heart-warming occurred. The door of the dressing-room opened, and in came a fellow Welshman, that fine golfer Dai Rees. We'd never exchanged a word, although Dai sometimes trained at Highbury. But now he came over to me, to say, "Well done, sonny. You've played your part in this."

Which brings me to two of our forwards who I have not previously mentioned. They, too, had something to do with our success; Peter Goring and, to a lesser degree, Reg Lewis, who was soon to retire.

I've always maintained that big, blond Peter burned himself out with the sheer exuberant energy of his performances during 1949-50. That season ended gloriously for him, with a fine display at Wembley and a cup winners' medal, but he was never again to show quite the same form. Later, of course, he converted with success to wing-half-back, but he'd chased himself silly before this; had worked himself to the bone for Arsenal. Later on, I was afraid that Derek Tapscott would do the same thing, but we managed to cool him down.

Peter's very quiet, but he's a good mixer. He just won't break into a conversation very easily. When a group is talking, Peter is usually the one who stands by and listens. He's a shrewd fellow, and a real golfing fanatic, who performs pretty creditably on the links. I believe his handicap is about twelve.

Reg was playing mostly in the reserves by this time, but he was still essentially a First Division player of high order, which was once shown by a match against Luton Town reserves. The score was a surprising 5-5, Reg having got two of ours, and there were only a few minutes to go. He had been strolling through the match, flicking the ball with head and foot. "Reg'll get another goal," I said confidently, to a fellow defender. And sure enough he did, a cracking third, just as good as the other two. A fine footballer, Reg.

The league and the season "proper" over, there was still the Coronation Cup to be competed for, in Glasgow. It turned out to be rather a triumph for Scottish teams, two of which won through to the final, and Arsenal went out in the first match, to Glasgow Celtic.

The only goal came from a corner kick, little Bobby Collin's effort swirling directly into the net, past George Swindin. At that very juncture, Tom Whittaker, sitting near me, leaned across, tapped me on, the knee, and said, "Get yourself fit for our tour." At that moment, I knew I had at last won my place as regular first-team goalkeeper, but I rather wish that George, not I, had played in our match against Rapid (Vienna), shortly afterwards.

The game took place in Bruges (Belgium) in oppressive heat which may have had something to do with our depressing performance, for we lost to the brilliant, green-shirted Austrians 6-1 and were made to look like selling platers. Their football, intricate, close-passing, built on sheer mastery of the ball, left us standing. They soon found that their right-winger had the beating of Lionel Smith, and they played remorselessly on our weak flank. Time and again, their winger beat him (I believe it was one of the famous Koerner brothers), cut along the by-line, and pulled the ball back for his inside-forward to run on to, and hit, at goal.

Personally, I was more upset about the number of the goals, that the way I let them through. In all honesty, I did not think there was very much I could do about them. We were rather an old side, it was a diabolically hot day – and Rapid were very good.

All the same, it made a strange, sad postscript to our championship season.

6
CONFETTI AND RED DRAGONS

Nineteen fifty-three-four was quite a season for me. Not only was I married, but I won my first international cap for Wales. What's more, I heard and enjoyed that news on the very day of my wedding.

I'd like to talk about my wife first. We met, very appropriately, at one of those pleasant dances organized by the Arsenal Supporter's Club, in 1951. It took place at Islington Town Hall, and the queer thing is (though not so queer, perhaps, in this coincidence bedevilled career of mine) that I ought not really to have gone at all. I don't dance, but the supporters rightly expect us to put in an appearance, and I was more than willing to do so.

Myrtle was a Spurs supporter then, but I'm thankful to say I soon changed that. I took her home after the dance that night; and I didn't ask to take her home – I told her! From that evening, it was a question of "going steady" for me, until our eventual marriage, nearly two and a half years later. By the grace of good fortune, Myrtle had been brought to the Arsenal dance, despite professing a rival "religion", by friends of hers from the King's Cross office where she worked as a secretary.

From the very first, Myrtle's father put no objection in our way. If ever I have met a man who is football crackers, then this is he. There are many analogies with my own father, except Myrtle's went in for the game in a bigger way. He has served in all three arms of the Forces, and Myrtle was actually born at R.A.F. Uxbridge. He played every form of sport, including football, refereed, ran teams, and organized in particular an R.A.F. team for which my mother-in-law played the same sterling part as did my mother, for Winch Wen. He's now pensioned off from R.A.F. maintenance, works in the office of a carpet factory, but lives a much more dedicated existence as member of a referee's selection committee, in Worcestershire. I'm happy to say that he was delighted to meet me, and there was no trouble at all about getting his consent.

"You couldn't wish to marry anybody better than a footballer," he told Myrtle, "provided he's a steady type, and knows what he's doing." Apparently I qualified. My father-in-law did not support any team in particular then, but now he is Arsenal crazy.

His wife is not only a great help to football teams, but she has a formidable sense of fun. There was the time, for instance, when some joker flew one of her undergarments from a flagpole in the R.A.F. barracks. In revenge, my mother-in-law took advantage of her position as unpaid, official laundress and kit inspector for the team. She sewed lace on the shorts of every player, and a bright red heart on the goalkeeper's jersey! Then the lace came off, but the bedazzled goalkeeper continued to wear his heart....

Myrtle and I were married at Swansea on 22 March, 1954 and it also happened to be the day on which the Welsh team to meet Ireland was due to be announced.

Earlier in the season, my name had been mentioned by one or two sports' writers as a possible for the Welsh eleven, in which Bill Shortt appeared to have ended his long and distinguished reign. But then Ronnie Howells of Cardiff was clearly in the running, too, and when the place did, in fact, go to him against England, I was not too disappointed. In fact I sent him a wire of congratulation, which he reciprocated when I was chosen. My feeling was that I was just a youngster, and that there was plenty of time and chance.

Thus, at my wedding reception, I was a little distracted, waiting for the news. The secretary of Winch Wen, who was a guest, kept ringing the local paper, to find out whether there was any news. Then at last an uncle of mine, who fancied himself as a bit of a humorist, came into the room and killed the party stone dead by announcing, "Hard luck, son, Howells is playing, again."

I felt a bit dejected, because I badly wanted to be chosen, on my wedding day. Later on, at home, we turned the radio on, and I listened with half an ear to hear the sad news confirmed. Instead, the first name that came out (this is perhaps the one advantage of being a goalkeeper) was...KELSEY. Pandemonium, of course, and I just couldn't stick it. It had all just overwhelmed me, and there were tears in my eyes as I walked out of the room.

The full team was: Kelsey; Sullivan (Cardiff); Sherwood (Cardiff); Paul (Swansea Town); Daniel (Sunderland); Burgess (Spurs); Foulkes (Newcastle); Kinsey (Birmingham); Charles (Leeds); Allchurch, I. (Swansea Town); Clarke (Manchester City).

You'll have noticed that the team included two of my own Swansea heroes, which made it all the more of a thrill. Another Swansea hero of mine at that time was not able to play. About him my feelings have since changed for...I ceased personally to idolize him when he sued another footballer.

The match against Ireland was, as always, a mid-week affair, and I duly reported at the Marine Hotel, Rhyl, at seven o'clock on the preceding Monday. I was the solitary new cap. Ronnie Burgess, the tireless Spurs left-half, was there to greet me, in his capacity as skipper. "Nice to have you with us," he told me, as if he really meant it, "and I hope you do well." Ronnie, whom I rated a good captain, nearly didn't play. An injured toe threatened to keep him out of the match, but injections luckily made it possible for him to take part.

Getting into the new crowd was not too easy at first, and I was grateful that I knew Ray Daniel, a seasoned Welsh campaigner by now, despite his extreme youth. Not that people were not friendly; in fact the first words I heard from one distinguished player were, "Come down to the bar!"

Down below, the lads were playing snooker, and my initiation took place smoothly enough, through joining in the game. I've always found that the finest way for a strange side to shake down is when it travels together. You simply cannot help but get to know one another, like that. On this occasion, there wasn't the chance, and I may add that we individuals had to travel up to Rhyl second-class, which was rather a surprise to me. Arsenal always travelled first.

Quite apart from personal acquaintanceship, there was little chance to get together on the field. We were limited to a single training session, which wasn't so bad for me, as goalkeeper, but could not have given the others all the team practice that they really needed.

In charge of the team was Mr. Herbert Powell, the secretary of the Welsh F.A., a quiet, religious man, non-smoking, non-drinking, be-in-bed-by-nine-thirty. But you could see he had a bit of authority, and when he did open his mouth, he was quite a forceful type of man. He would never tolerate heavy smoking or the "quiet drink" among the players.

I suppose one would describe him as an administrator, rather than a tactician. When Jimmy Murphy, the Manchester United trainer, was appointed team manager, Mr. Powell's authority was supplemented by tactical guidance, as well.

It was quite a thrill for me to meet Roy Paul, the man whose cultured football I had so admired when I was a kid, visiting the Vetch Field ground to see Swansea Town play. Roy looks a typical Rhondda Valley Welshman; they're a toughish bunch, and the dark-haired Roy gives the impression that he's fully capable of taking care of himself, on or off a football field.

Then there was John Charles; a big, quiet fellow, usually lurking about somewhere in the background. I sympathized with him, for I'm something like John, in this respect; quiet, until I really get to know people. In our case, two Quiet Men met, and stood there like a couple of dummies. But it wasn't long before we got to know one another fairly well. Nowadays, I know all the boys well, and if there's any mischief, I've probably started it!

I roomed with Cardiff's sturdy Alf Sherwood, who had been a pillar of the Welsh team for so long. We got on very well. "Don't worry about international matches," Alf advised, "just think it's an ordinary club match at Highbury and it'll be all right. Play your usual game."

Rather to my surprise, Alf went to bed at about half past nine, and I followed him at once, thinking that I must not take liberties on the occasion of my first cap. But instead of putting out the light, Alf got into bed with a book and read...and read...and read, till midnight. I was to find that this is Alf's special method of knocking himself out and sleeping without difficulty. I never find any trouble about getting to sleep, which is one of my good points, I suppose; the only difficulty is in waking up....

Next morning we had a team meeting, at which we discussed each Irish player in turn. I was told to keep a special eye on Peter McParland, the Aston Villa outside-left, who was also playing in his first international. He was a big, tall fellow who was especially dangerous in the air, when crosses came floating in from the other wing. Then there was Eddie McMorran the former Belfast blacksmith, who was also in the Irish attack. "Watch him whenever you gather the ball," I was told, "and get rid of it was quickly as possible. McMorran has a habit of going for the goalkeeper, and if you aren't quick, you'll find yourself and the ball in the back of the net." So I promised I would be careful.

We trained that morning on the Rhyl ground; just a few laps and a kick-about, with nothing really constructive or tactical, though Jimmy Murphy has changed all that. In the afternoon, we went to the cinema and visited a youth club, where we met the youngsters, played table tennis, and generally "mucked in".

That evening, we were told we could have breakfast in bed if we wanted it – and I certainly did! I reckoned that I needed all the rest I could get. The kick-off was in the evening, and we seemed to spend much of the intervening time signing shoals of autograph books, coming in from people who had heard that we were staying at the Marine Hotel. In the afternoon, we went to bed again until about four o'clock, then came down for a meal of steak or cold chicken. I stuck to the habitual steak-and-toast, in good Arsenal fashion. Habits among clubs vary a good deal on this score, however; some have eggs and sherry, others prefer to give their players glucose and milk. So long as it isn't heavy, I suppose that is the main thing. After the meal, off we went in the coach, to the Racecourse Ground.

There were twenty-seven telegrams waiting for me in the dressing-room, but just as I was about to open them, someone bellowed at me to stop. "It's unlucky," I was told. "You must not open them on any account, until afterwards." Maybe they're right, I thought – we pro footballers are all pretty superstitious. After all, I opened the telegrams before the Charlton match, and look what happened to me then.

The ground was filled nearly to capacity by a crowd of about 32,000, but I must say it hardly seemed a fit arena for an international match. The dressing-rooms were stuck away in a corner of the stadium, and as for the pitch, I'd noticed when watching a match there in my army days that it rose and fell a little alarmingly. Now, trotting out on to the pitch to play there myself, I found it bumpy; it's goal mouths grassless as this late stage of the season.

After a mere forty seconds from the kick off, I thought to myself, "Back to Charlton." I had already let through a goal. Peter McParland, that goalkeepers' nightmare, scored it. He received the ball out on the left, near the touch-line, about twelve yards inside our half. He worked his way in towards the edge of the penalty-box, while our defence covered up quickly, expecting a cross. Instead, Peter sent a long lob into the goal mouth; a lob that seemed to be going harmlessly over the bar. I said, *seemed*. In fact, just as we were all turning round in preparation for the kick, the powerful wind caught the ball and blew it into the net, in the top far corner. It was, by the way, the first time Peter had touched the ball, and my first touch was when I took it out of the net.

It wasn't a great game, for the bumpy pitch spoiled the football. McParland scored another, to put us two down, and John Charles dashed through to notch a consolation mark for us. A clearance of mine passed over their centre-half's head, John rounded him, beat him for pace, and smashed the ball home.

Eddie McMorran fulfilled predictions by having a "go" at me. I'll wait for the next time, I told myself, and tuck my shoulder into him. And when the next time came, so I did. In the hotel that night, however, the referee, Scotland's Charlie Faultless, told me, "I could have given a foul against you, for playing the man," an observation which has had me thinking ever since.

McMorran also gave me the chance to make a rather spectacular save. He was up to a high centre and nodded the ball down. It was going inside the post, about a foot high from the ground, but I flung myself across, and managed to turn it round the post.

If I haven't got a great deal to say about this match, perhaps it was because the atmosphere was so dead that one might not have been taking part in an international at all. From my point of view, I suppose that was not a bad thing. It would certainly have been pretty hard to make one's debut in the frenziedly keen atmosphere of Cardiff, with national passions running as high as the grandstand. Up north, you don't get the mad valley boys, who are worth a goal start at Ninian Park.

On the other hand, the Scots always have a secret weapon when they come down to play at Cardiff – their own supporters. We stay at the Angel Hotel, opposite the castle, and the fans arrive in their special trains round about six or seven in the morning. Thus it is that one wakes up to a din of Scots voices and Scots rattles – and even Scots bagpipes, which is a little bit much at that early hour. It probably helps their side, I've often thought, by losing us a few hours sleep!

I was fairly satisfied with the game I'd played against Ireland, though of course it was disappointing to have lost. Sherwood told me he thought I had done fairly well for a first game, and the selectors let me know that they were satisfied.

At all events, I was retained for the close-season match, the following May, against Austria, in Vienna. With memories of what Rapid had done to Arsenal the year before, I knew it was not going to be very easy, but the prospect of the trip was a thrill. Vienna was the farthest that I had so far travelled.

We flew via Zurich to the little airport at Vienna, where there was a group of R.A.F. boys to give us a welcome, and a broadcaster to interview us. Vienna, I found, was a terrific place. The main opera house was still under reconstruction but the city-tour on which we were taken showed us one splendid building after another; I particularly remember the church of St.

Stephen's with its spire, and a fine old castle up on a hill, overlooking the city.

We were all walking about in its courtyard when somebody all of a sudden spotted a big Alsatian dog, up on the wall. It gave a ferocious bark, and looked as if it were just about to jump down among us. I'm ashamed to admit that we players dashed away in all directions, which prompted a selector to the dry remark, "If we move as fast as this in the match, the Austrians will never catch us."

With us in our trips around Vienna went three young Welsh lads from the Rhondda Valley. They had saved up specially to make the journey, and we took them wherever we went. One visit was to a British barracks, where we had a wonderful evening. John Charles shed his diffidence, took the microphone, and gave an impression of Billy Daniels. John is full of beans, when you get him going. Derek Tapscott is full of beans whether you do or not.

Young Derek, who had joined Arsenal from Barry Town during the previous season, came in right at the end to score twice against Liverpool, then a couple more against Portsmouth. The Welsh selectors were so impressed that they chose him for his first international. Derek never stops talking. I remember him at the barracks party, standing on the sofa in his stockinged feet, and giving one imitation after another, into the mike.

Out team manager was none other than Walley Barnes, who kept the job until he joined BBC Television, when the Welsh F.A. apparently thought it a little hard that Walley might be called upon publicly to criticize himself! He had a nasty shock the evening that he took us all to the Moulin Rouge night club to listen to the music and watch the dancing. He had us all very decorously settled, up in the balcony, with a glass of lemon juice apiece. When the bill came he very nearly collapsed; the tiny wineglasses of lemon had cost him nearly six shillings apiece, and we practically had to carry him out!

The match took place in the Peter Stadium, which was in the Russian zone. One noticed a lot of Russian soldiers at the match, which I still believe to be one of the best that Wales have ever played. True, we lost 2-0, true the Austrians weren't really at their best, especially with regard to shooting. Nevertheless, you can't take the credit from Wales. We played a lot of good football that day.

We went into the match with a plan. In training, Walley had worked out with us a number of tactical moves, but our primary aim was to make good use of the wings. Cliff Jones of Swansea Town was on our left flank, and our aim was to make use of his speed, giving him the ball as much as possible. In the event, the scheme did not work very well. Under the close marking Austrian tactics, an Austrian defender sat on Cliff for most of the game, and he seldom had the chance to break away.

In midfield, I suppose we were outplayed, and the 70,000 Austrian fans were able to cheer some pretty Viennese School movements. The man who stood out above everyone else was Ernst Ocwirk, whose role could best be described, perhaps, as that of wandering wing-half. This was the period in which the Austrian team was forsaking the classic methods of defence and going over, a little shakily, to the stopper centre-half and wing-halves playing in the middle of the field.

Ocwirk, a dark, strapping fellow, seemed to cover the whole of the pitch. He took your eye again and again, and his passing and heading were fine. But although he gave his forwards a fine service, and although Dienst, in the middle of the attack, was always quick and dangerous, the Austrians did not shoot very often. Maybe it's because I always like to have a lot of work to do, but nurse a sort of grudge against continental teams, on this account.

We should have scored an equalizing goal, and if we had, maybe the result would have been very different. With the Austrians a goal up, blond Ivor Allchurch raced after a through pass, ran round the centre-half, and took the ball up to the goalkeeper. It looked odds on a goal, as Ivor ran up to the goalkeeper. But he who hesitates is lost, and the goalie had just that fractional chance which he needed, to block the ball at Ivor's feet.

It was really fatal. The goalkeeper at once cleared the ball up-field to his outside-right, a quick scissors movement took the Austrians through our defence, and the final return pass was crashed into goal by the forward who had made all the running. I don't think I had very much chance with that one; and we were two down.

Meanwhile, we were not down-hearted, and were playing plenty of good, straightforward football on our own account. Afterwards, many Austrians said it was the best game they had ever seen in Vienna, which is quite a compliment when you think of the pre-war days of the Wunderteam. Big John Charles was like a rock at centre-half, and Derek Tapscott was doing very well in his first international. I don't know where Derek gets his energy from, for after all, there isn't a great deal of him. He is the sort of person who will always rather be moving around than sitting still, and there were times when his quick bursts certainly had the Austrians worried.

On one occasion, he was involved in what turned into a very nasty incident. He and Trevor Ford went for the Austrian goalkeeper on his goal-line, always a dubious thing to do in front of a continental crowd. The goalie finished hanging upside-down in the netting, and the ball went with him, but the "goal" was disallowed for a foul against Wales.

From the free kick, the Austrians moved right down into our penalty-area. One of them came running towards John

Charles and to my horror and astonishment, he seemed to make little effort to play the ball, the studs of his boots landing right in John's thigh. Poor John went down like a log, and when Jack Jones of Wrexham, our trainer, came on to examine him, it was to find six great black marks on his powerful thigh. Yet John never said a word to anyone. He just got to his feet, went on playing, and never even attempted to retaliate. It was a copybook example of great sportsmanship, under appalling provocation.

There was the usual crowd resentment over the way I took my goal kicks; a hailstorm of whistling every time I ran up to the dead ball. If I tapped it to the back, and picked up the return pass, that was all right, just as it had been in Paris. Once I decided to kid them. I took my usual run-up, to the familiar aviary of whistling, came to the ball – and stopped dead. That seemed to amuse them, but it did not prevent them from giving me the bird on every subsequent occasion that I took a kick in my way. There's a strange lack of tolerance about this attitude, I feel. British crowds to not jeer foreign goalkeepers for patting the ball outside the area to a back, though this way of taking goal kicks is just as strange to us as our own method appear to be, to them.

So we lost this game, but it was still a match to be remembered.

There was an amusing moment, during our wanderings round Vienna, when Derek Tapscott fancied an ashtray on a stall, which appeared to be marked seven shillings. "Let's see," said Trevor Ford, who had noticed him examining it, and Derek handed it over. "Good," said Trevor, "I think I'll have this." He handed it to the woman in charge of the stall – to discover that the price was not seven shillings but nineteen. It was too late to back down, and Trevor had to pay up.

On the way home, passing through the Customs, one of our players played a rather novel trick. He had bought a glass bowl, which he was carrying in a package under his arm. When we stopped once more at Zurich airport, he fancied a clock, and he bought that, too. At the London Airport Customs, he was asked what he was carrying under each arm. "Oh," he replied, "I've bought a glass bowl, which you can put water in."

"That's all right," said the Customs officer, "and what about the other parcel."

"That," said the player, blandly, "is the base you put the bowl on."

After the trip I was able to spend the summer quietly with Myrtle. I shall never forget the first meal she cooked for me. "What would you like when we arrive back in London?" she had asked me, and I had replied, "Oh, knock me up a bit of a grill."

Alas, when we arrived in our house, which the club had kindly provided, the cooker hadn't arrived, and Myrtle was obliged to borrow a portable electric cooker. The grill took her three hours, poor girl, and it nearly broke her heart.

Myrtle comes to every Arsenal home match, and she really knows the game; nor does she miss international matches in which I'm involved, if she can possible help it. She is perhaps my biggest critic, pulls me to pieces without mercy, and sometimes, in my humble opinion, even takes it a little too far! I often say to her, "If you think you can do better, there's the jersey – carry on." She takes care of all my cuttings, which I would otherwise be too lazy to look after, myself. One point on which she often attacks me is if I dive at the feet of an advancing forward, and only manage to block the ball, instead of holding it.

"You're miles too slow," says Myrtle. "You should have got out and held it, you're not supposed to block it." And if I drop a cross I've really "had it".

"With hands that size," says Myrtle, "you should be ashamed of yourself." Perhaps it is just as well that her father is the precise opposite; he will never hear a word said against me. If I fumble a centre, far from taking me to task, he will say, "Jack was hustled off the ball – he couldn't have dropped a cross." Somewhere between the two opinions, no doubt, reality lies....

I'm afraid that I just will not let my mother-in-law come to matches in which I'm playing, for I am convinced that somehow she brings me bad luck; I always seem to have a bad game whenever she turns up. I broke a finger once at St. Andrew's, when she was watching our match against Birmingham, and did it again at The Hawthorns, when she was present at a game against West Bromwich. When we met Albion there in the cup, in 1956, I'm afraid I would not even give her a ticket! "You get into the ground if you can," I said, "but I'm not going to let you have a pass." That may sound very unkind of me, but surely we are all entitled to our own pet superstitions. Whether or not they have any real basis, the fact is that they can often work on a footballer's sensibilities and cause him to have a bad game, just because he believes in them.

On that occasion, my poor mother-in-law, determined to see the match by hook or by crook, went on to the terraces and stood.

As a footballer's wife, Myrtle sometimes has to answer the door to some odd visitors. Once, she found two young lads on the doorstep. "Somebody told us a famous footballer lives here," one of them said. "Could we have his autograph?"

"Have you brought your autograph books or some paper?" Myrtle inquired.

"No, we haven't got either," was the answer. "But you tell us what his name is, and we'll write it down when we get home."

Another time, when I was out, a boy called who wanted to know where he could write to Tom Whittaker. When Myrtle asked him why, he replied that he wanted to play for Arsenal.

"You're too young," Myrtle told him.

"I know," said the boy, quite unperturbed. "But if I write to him now, I can go and join the Arsenal as soon as I leave school."

There's nothing like optimism, I suppose.

7
RETREAT FROM MOSCOW

If my views on the matter are of any interest, I still believe that Arsenal should never have made the trip to Moscow which resulted in a disastrous beating at the hands of the famous Dynamo, on an early October day in 1954. Still, it's history now, not very encouraging history from a Highbury point of view, and I suppose it's a little late to complain.

This, however, I must say. To play a match of this nature, you must be 100 per cent fit; a fact which nobody can sanely deny. And our team, when it took the field at the Dynamo Stadium, wasn't in condition to play a game of draughts, let alone a game of football. It was not our fault...but let me start at the beginning.

To begin with, despite the fact that our match against Dynamo was on a Tuesday, the Football League quite inexplicably refused us permission to cancel our league game against Leicester City on the Saturday. British prestige, apparently, took a bad second place to our parochial, all-the-year-round competition. So we were forced to travel to Leicester on the Saturday, play Dynamo on Tuesday, leave Moscow for London, quit London on Friday for Sheffield, and play yet a third match against the Wednesday, at Hillsborough, the following day. This meant a round trip of about 3,500 miles, in eight days. Anybody would have been welcome to change places with me. I wonder if the youngster who wanted to join the Arsenal straight from school would have been quite so keen, if he had been on this wearying trip.

This Dynamo match was bound to be a needle match from the start. In 1945, the Dynamos had played a mixed Arsenal team, full of guest players, in the fog at Tottenham, and had beaten it 4-3, in what I understood to have been very suspicious circumstances. The two clubs had never met, before or since, and the Gunners had never before been invited to Moscow. Oddly enough, our team included one player who had played and, played brilliantly, against the 1945 Dynamos. Big Tommy Lawton had then been leading the Chelsea attack, a man at his peak, and he had given their defence quite a chasing, I understood, when Chelsea had drawn 3-3 with the Russians in their opening match, at Stamford Bridge. Tommy had just joined us from Brentford, where he had a spell as player-manager.

Staying over Saturday night at the Coburg Hotel, we were called next morning at the appalling hour of five-thirty, had a light breakfast of a boiled egg and toast, then were off by coach for Northolt Airport. We had a wonderful send-off, despite the early hour, with photographers, newsreel and television cameras and airport officials all waiting for us. Two B.E.A. Vikings were to fly us to Prague, and there was a reason for this.

In May 1949, a disaster shook the whole of the soccer world, when seventeen members of the Torino football club perished in an air crash at Superga, behind the city, and Italy lost almost her complete team. Arsenal did not want to take such a risk; hence the use of two aircraft, instead of one.

Our first stop (my plane included Sir Bracewell Smith, Sir Stanley Rous, the F.A. secretary, and the Governor) was at Frankfurt. On the way we ran into a few air pockets, and the consequent rocking and rolling led several of the boys to refuse the meal which was served. They regretted it later, for we did not get another bite to eat until we arrived at Minsk, at one o'clock the following morning, apart from coffee at Frankfurt, and tea and (inedible) biscuits on the Russian plane.

The second stop was Prague, and it was at this point that the trip became intriguing. The captain of our aeroplane had told us that he must at all costs cross the Iron Curtain within minutes of a certain time, otherwise we were liable to be "buzzed" by MiG fighters; who would ensure that our aircraft kept within the mile wide permissible "corridor" all the way to Prague airport. He managed it, and there were no difficulties.

I don't think any of us was much impressed by the aerodrome at Prague. There was hardly any sign of activity, and apart from the Vikings which had brought us, the only sign of activity to be seen was provided by a couple of light training aircraft. Compared with London Airport, Prague Airport looked like a little farm out in the Wild West, though in fairness I must say that it was greatly improved, when I landed there a couple of years later, for Wales' match against Czechoslovakia.

In a moment of abstraction, I raised my camera to take a photograph – but we weren't in the West any more. An airport official promptly came up from behind to knock down my arm, telling me that this sort of thing was strictly out of court. There was nothing to do but pass a dreary hour in the airport lounge, looking half-heartedly at old Polish, German, Czech and Russian newspapers, before the Russian Aeroflots arrived.

I didn't like the look of these at all. They seemed old and battered, and I seriously doubted whether they would survive the trip to Moscow. There were not even any seat belts, and the seats themselves were far from comfortable. The only consolation was that our Aeroflot did boast a table, on which we were able to carry on with a game of cards. What a table it was, too. Nothing modern about this Aeroflot; the piece of furniture might have come straight out of some old-fashioned farmhouse kitchen. But Tom Lawton, Alex Forbes, Walley Barnes and I made a bee-line for it. It was a friend in need.

We were in the front of the Aeroplane, and running along the side was an ancient couch, the springs of which were sticking through the material. We gathered that this was meant as a haven and refuge for those in peril in the air and, sure enough, Alex Forbes was soon making use of it.

Though our first stop was intended to be Minsk, we came down for some unfathomable reason at Warsaw; perhaps to refuel, for we were only there for about twenty minutes. We were then told that our next stop would be Moscow, but it proved to be another red herring. When we saw lights below us, we assumed this must be the capital, but the stewardess who did not speak a word of English, made us understand that this was Minsk. Two hours passed, again there were lights below us, again we asked the stewardess whether this was Moscow at last. No, she told us, to our astonishment, it was....Minsk. It was the modern equivalent of those infinite stories about Russians trundling across Siberia in trains. Apparently the pilot had received a radio message from Moscow that it was under a blanket of fog, and that it would consequently be dangerous to land. Hence, we had turned back to Minsk.

We hung around there for hours, hoping to receive the go-ahead from Moscow, but at half past two in the morning, it was decided that we should remain for the night. Nobody seemed to have any idea of where we could be lodged, and we players were so tired that several of us tried to snatch a quick nap in the airport lounge. One or two of the lads used the ends of the long, draped curtains to keep them warm.

Al last it was decided that the number two party could be accommodated at an hotel, but so far as the number one party, which, alas, was mine, was concerned, it must sleep in what turned out to be a communal dormitory. We were driven into Minsk by car, arriving at a building which no doubt was a cheap hostel, but looked to me from outside rather like a working-man's club. Our party was divided between two rooms, and when we arrived in ours, it was to find that there were some thirty beds in it.

This didn't appeal to us at all, and we said so forcibly, but Sir Stanley Rous and Tom Whittaker calmed us down by admonishing us, "Now, lads, if it's good enough for us, it's good enough for you." So we each picked out a bed, and climbed in a quietly as possible, to avoid disturbing the sleeping Russians. I remember Tom Lawton and Alex Forbes pulling out the cabinet which stood between their beds, presumably so that they might give each other moral support, should anything go wrong.

When Alex was undressing, he neatly folded his trousers so that they should not crease, turning them upside-down to do so. At once all his loose change fell to the floor with a clatter, and there was a horrified, frozen moment as we stood waiting for the Russians to wake. They didn't at first, but one coin seemed to roll round and round for ages like a possessed humming-top, and by the time it stopped, we could hear several disgruntled Russians muttering away to themselves. Suddenly, to our astonishment, one of them got out of bed, walked out of the room with a fixed stare, and marched back to bed again. I assumed he must be walking in his sleep, or perhaps he was just inordinately fond of exercise.

After a mere and miserable three hours sleep, trainer Billy Milne was shaking us out of our slumbers. We were driven, bleary eyed, back to that infernal airport, got into the planes again, and flew off to Moscow, this time with no mishaps. I've heard it suggested that the Russians planned this jaunt in Minsk; that they have long memories, and recalled that when the Dynamos arrived in London in 1945, they were lodged at first in Guards' barracks with mould on the walls, before moving out in disgust. Perhaps there's some truth in it.

If so, they certainly took an ample revenge, obliging our F.A. secretary and one of Britain's most distinguished managers to doss down in such unappetizing conditions.

At Moscow, we were given a traditional Russian welcome, each member of the party receiving a huge bouquet of flowers, after which we were shown into a large room at the airport, where members of the Russian F.A. made speech of welcome.

The journey into Moscow by coach was very, very drab. There was not much sign of life until we got to the outskirts of the city, and even there the dwellings of the Moscovites seemed to consist of dirty wooden huts. The fact that it was raining heavily, so that these huts were ankle deep in mud, probably made our impression bleaker. But Moscow itself turned out to be very different; a city of many wonderful buildings.

When we got to the National Hotel, our one thought was bed, as quickly as possible and, as soon as we were awake again – food. Our first lunch, however, was rather disconcerting. It consisted of a boneless chicken leg, filled with butter, and cooked in a batter surround. As soon as we tried to cut this with a knife, the butter oozed and squirted in all directions, as though from some berserk toothpaste tube. That chef must have been quite a practical joker. In addition, the food was too rich for our stomachs still disturbed by the journey, and we asked if we could possibly have our good old English steak-and-chips.

It transpired that we could – not only for that meal, but for every other lunch and dinner we ate, for the remainder of our stay. There was plenty of caviar, too, and wines and vodka, which were, of course, forbidden to us completely, until after the match, when we sampled a little.

After lunch, all of us feeling a lot better for the food and the sleep, we drove off in a taxi for the first sight of the Dynamo Stadium, to accustom ourselves to it, and to do a spot of training. The vastness of the ground was impressive. It holds 100,000 people, for 90,000 of whom there is seating accommodation. On one side of the stadium there is a huge monument to Lenin and Stalin, whose faces are carved in stone. There's a first-class running track around the field which was being used by Soviet athletes, while we trained. The most notable of them was Irene Terova, who was then, I am told, the second fastest woman in the Soviet Union over 100 metres. She could certainly have given us a few yards over the distance.

It was still raining very heavily when we arrived at the stadium, and we were naturally most surprised to find that for all that, the playing pitch was as dry as a bone. Later we were to realize why. As soon as rain begins to fall, groundsmen rush out to cover the pitch with four immense tarpaulins, rather on the lines of the precautions which are taken at Wimbledon tennis tournaments. I'd very much like to see this done at our British soccer grounds, and there might be an end to clubs grumbling about the state of the pitch. It would mean that we should be playing, week after week, on pitches which are more or less the same consistency, no matter what the weather conditions, and I'm sure that this would benefit the soccer standards.

Though most people seem to regard us British footballers as chameleons in our adaptability, I personally would far prefer to play regularly on dry grounds; and surely every club in the Football League can afford the price of four tarpaulins.

The Dynamo Stadium is magnificent inside, as well as out. Instead of the tiled walls which we have at Highbury, its own walls are covered with modern and very decorative wallpaper, and the floors have thick carpets. This motif of luxury is kept up with easy chairs for players to sit on, instead of benches or forms, and coat stands on which to hang one's clothes, instead of the customary pegs. The entrance to the ground is decorated with paintings of sporting events.

It was early to bed for us that night. We had been invited to see the Bolshoi ballet perform *Swan Lake*, which would have been a considerable thrill. But Tom Whittaker decided that the show ran too late.

Approaching the ground, on the following afternoon, it seemed to us that the entire population of Moscow must be going to the match. Certainly it was a wonderful sight to see how the police marshalled the crowds. They were never at any time allowed into the road, but had to keep strictly to the footpaths. Thousands of police, standing almost shoulder to shoulder, had cordoned the stadium, and if you could not produce a ticket, it was impossible to get by them.

We took the field, via an underground tunnel, twenty minutes before the kick-off, to give time for the speeches, the presentation of teams, and the playing of both national anthems, where photographs were taken, as well. Each member of the Dynamo team carried a large bouquet of flowers, and as soon as they had been handed to us, we Arsenal players broke away, made for different parts of the ground, and tossed them to the spectators, which probably got us our biggest cheer of the evening.

The preliminaries over, we were told to return to the dressing-rooms for a few minutes before the kick-off. Once again, it had been raining all day, and I don't think it stopped for a moment, throughout the time we were in Moscow. But the pitch, thanks to those tarpaulins, was in wonderful condition. Our team was: myself; Barnes; Wade; Goring;

Dickson; Forbes; Tapscott; Logie (captain); Lawton; Lishman and Roper.

Jimmy won the toss, Dynamo kicked off, and the game started with a series of strong Arsenal attacks. Alas, we had no success, and the giant Yashine's goal remained inviolate. It seemed to be anybody's game until a minute before half-time, when Dynamo broke away, there was a slight tangle in the Arsenal defence, and Ilyine, the Dynamos' international inside-forward, scored with a well-placed shot from about eight yards.

By now, it was raining so hard that the pitch was beginning to cut up a little, and I really hate to think what it would have been like had the ground not been covered, until shortly before the match. In the dressing-room at half-time, we were not greatly disturbed by the fact that we were a goal down, for the game had been very even, and we had certainly succeeded in holding our own.

Alas, we went to pieces in the second half, when the long trek we'd made and our lack of sleep began to take their toll. We tired badly, and it was only five minutes before the Dynamos, again through Ilyine, scored, making it Dynamo 2, Arsenal 0. Shortly after this, they had a glorious chance to be three up, when a penalty was given against us for some infringement, by the Czech referee Mr. Marko. Savduninx took it, and had he kept the ball six inches lower it would have been a perfect example of how a penalty should be shot. He side-footed the ball very firmly towards my top, left-hand corner, and I had no chance of getting it. But the ball, to my great relief, struck the angle of upright and crossbar, and bounced clear.

We were putting in the occasional attack, without causing their defence much anxiety. The way they moved the ball was a delight to watch, and they also looked the fittest side I have ever played against, though our own exhaustion might have contributed to this impression. Fifteen minutes from the end, Ryjkine sewed up the match by scoring their third goal, and from that point, it seemed to be all Dynamo.

Their young centre-forward, Mamedov, got another, a couple of minutes later, and it was a nap hand when Bill Dickson got in the way of a hard, low cross, which he deflected past me, off the post, two minutes from time. I don't think a team has ever been so glad to hear the final whistle as we were. I still believe that if we had been able to arrive earlier in Moscow, and spend a few days there before the game, we would have put up a very different exhibition.

Still, we could not have left too dismal an impression, for although it must have been a good couple of hours after the end of the game that we left the stadium, hundreds of people were waiting outside to give us a splendid cheer.

Apart from the result, our own indifferent performance had given me a double disappointment. I had been looking forward to seeing a really acrobatic performance by Yachine, in Dynamos' goal, a performance recalling the antics of the famous "Tiger" Khomich, who had been in Dynamos' goal when they visited England in 1945. "If he's like Khomich," I had told myself, "he'll take some beating." Alas, he was very rarely troubled.

Dynamo seemed to play fluid football, with no set plan. Their ball control was splendid, they interchanged a great deal in attack, and it was very hard for our defence to get on top of them. In defence they suffered from none of the fiddling which afflicts many a continental side, and gives their opponents second chances. They cleared first time, and passed as soon as they saw a man in the open space. The man who most caught my eye was their outside-right, who showed an unusual power of acceleration.

That evening we were the guests of honour at a banquet given for us by the Ministry of Sport, an occasion brightened by a concert. This over, we were asked if we would like to see the famous Moscow Metro, their equivalent of the London Transport underground. It was certainly impressive, spotlessly clean and beautifully lit. No smoking is allowed, from the moment you enter a station, every wall is marble, ornamented the whole length of the platform with mosaics, so that if it wasn't for the electric railway lines, you would think you were in the long hall of some modern palace. Certainly the decorations were a great change from the glaring poster of our own underground. The entrance hall to every station was presided over by an imposing figure of Stalin, though with the end of the "cult of personality", I don't know whether Big Brother will be watching the travellers any more.

We went to bed that night doing our best to forget about the game, and to concentrate on the pleasure of the next day, when we were to be taken on a tour of the Kremlin, for three hours.

On entering the Kremlin, our woman guide, who spoke perfect English, told us we could take photographs anywhere in the grounds, but not inside the building. Dave Bowen, our Welsh left-half, who was travelling-reserve for the trip, nearly got himself into trouble with his camera. He wanted to take a shot of a sentry standing at his post, and raised his camera to do so. But while Dave was getting the sentry in his camera sights, the sentry was getting Dave in the sights of his rifle....I don't think for one moment that he intended to deprive Wales of one of her most promising half-backs; he just did not like the idea of being photographed. Maybe he just didn't think he was photogenic.

I suppose you could call the Kremlin a city within a city. It is, of course, full of historical relics. We saw horse-drawn coaches, jewels, and arms, dating back to the Russian Empire's earliest days, and were fascinated by the wonderful church-like buildings within the great outer wall. One oddity was provided by a bell which is claimed by the Russians to be the largest in the world, and no doubt is.

The trouble with these tours, alas, is that one tries to see too much in too short a time, and this trip round the Kremlin was very tiring indeed, so much so that many of us began skipping different sights, so that we could take a rest. Fully to appreciate a place like the Kremlin, you need at the very least a couple of days.

Another distraction was provided by a shopping expedition, to the famous Goum store. British housewives, I am sure, would go crazy at the thought of having to shop in Moscow. The Goum store is a colossal building which has shops set on each side of its three-tiered corridors. There, you could buy anything you cared to think of, though the prices were stupendously high. The Russians had been kind enough to give us 1,000 roubles each in spending money, which they told us was the equivalent of £100. It might have been at their artificial rates of exchange, but when we got into the land of Goum, we found that it was worth no more than £20.

To buy anything, you first had to push your way through great crowds. These Russians seem to number window shopping among their favourite pastimes, and they gather in droves around shop-fronts. When you have picked out your article, you hand it to the girl behind the counter. She gives you a ticket in return which you must then take to another counter to pay; and this involves queuing, for the second time. Thus it boils down to the fact that for every article you buy you must be prepared for a fight through the crowd, followed by a wait in two queues. I really could not imagine British housewives putting up with this, for long.

That evening, our last in Moscow, we spent at the British Embassy, where, after an official reception, some of the officials laid on an informal reception of their own. We certainly appreciated it; it was good to be back again amongst English people. Though the people of Moscow had generally seemed very friendly towards us, the language difficulty was immense, for, apart from our interpreters, we did not meet a single English-speaking Russian.

Next day we flew back to England, and all of us, players and officials alike, raised a cheer when we saw the Vikings which would take us on the last stage, coming in to land at Prague Airport.

When we reached London Airport, we were considerably surprised. A Customs officer blandly asked us, "Who has got the two clocks, and which of you has the tricycle and silver cups?"

Unknown to us, a list of the presents which we'd purchased had already appeared in the London newspapers. A certain reporter had asked us in the normal course of conversation what we had bought, and then decided that it would make a good story. Apparently it had been good enough to interest this Customs officer. I hope that journalist will realise the spot he might have put us in, if we hadn't declared our purchases. The clocks, you see, were mine. Joe Wade had bought the tricycle for his son, Robert, while the silver cups were Tommy Lawton's.

When Alex Forbes was asked if he had anything to declare, he answered, "Three tons of caviar."

In November, we faced another Russian team, this time at Highbury. Spartak, who, with Dynamo, monopolized the honours in Russian football, were due to kick off a brief tour of England with a match against us, and go on to Wolverhampton for a second game. Both would take place under floodlights. We were not playing terribly well at the time, whereas Spartak had been on a real goal spree in Belgium, and had received a terrific build-up from those of our journalists who'd been over there to take a look at them before they arrived in England. To tell the truth, I was a little bit worried about what might happen.

In the event, I need hardly have worried, for Spartak were most disappointing, and were very lucky to beat us. We had young Jim Fotheringham playing what was only his second first team game for us, at centre-half, and he had to mark the much publicized Simonian. Though Simonian got both Spartak's goals, Jim saw to it that he did very little else, and gave a most competent performance, I thought.

Before the match, Tom Whittaker had shown us a picture of the Spartak team and, pointing at their moustached goalkeeper, Piraev, had remarked, "Look at that fellow; his arms come down to his knees!" So they did. This Piraev, in fact, used his long, gangling arms to keep goal in a typically spectacular continental manner, though they weren't long enough or quick enough to prevent Jimmy Logie from opening the score for us.

It was a wet night and a white ball. The ground had cut up quite a bit, and in the conditions, Spartak's short passing game came unstuck.

It was one of those days on which it was dangerous to hold the ball, and they equalized when I could do no more than push out a shot to the edge of the six-yard box. I was just getting up from the crowd as the ball came to Simonian, and though I threw myself at his feet, he was too quick for me, and shot the ball home to make the score 1-1.

Simonian gave his side the lead when a cross from the right-wing found him unmarked on the six-yard area, and he barely had to jump to head the ball into the goal.

That goal was, as it transpired, the winner, but it never should have been. Arthur Milton got away on one of his inspired bursts from the right-wing, outstripped the field, moved into the Russian penalty area, and was in such a position that it would have been harder to have missed than to have scored. But the Russian left-back, who had been faintly pursuing, tackled him from behind, took his legs and up-ended him. It looked to be to be the clearest penalty I've ever seen in my life, but we did not get it – there was a Russian referee.

What's more, he was none other than Nicolai Latyshev, the man who had charge of Arsenal's celebrated fog-farce against the Dynamos! It was pretty cool of Spartak to bring him back, but no doubt they relied on the probability that passions had cooled and memories had faded. Certainly it was tolerant of Arsenal to accept him, after being once bitten. Yet the fact remains that he *is* a very good referee. He took charge of our match in Leipzig against East Germany, a couple of years later, and made an almost perfect job of it.

It was this penalty incident which led to a sad and unpleasant sequel. The referee went up to Jimmy Logie, at the end of the game, and offered to shake hands with him. Jimmy, still very upset at the appalling penalty decision, refused, and was seen to refuse by one of the directors. Apparently, he could never forgive Jimmy for this. At Christmas-time, when he saw and shook hands with all the players, he left Jimmy out. Perhaps it was unintentional, but it certainly had affected him.

As for Spartak, they disappointed me, and I believe that our team of today would beat them. Only the blond Igor Netto, left-half and captain of Russia, really impressed me, with his clever passes and sixth-forward forays. They were in luck that evening.

8
A LESSON FROM EUROPE

It's odd how footballers are so often just about the last to know they've been "honoured". Just as I learned from a newspaper that I was about to make my league debut (and it was someone else's newspaper, at that!), so it was from a paper that I heard of my selection for the Great Britain side to play The Rest of Europe.

The month was August, 1955, and the match, as you'll probably remember, was scheduled to celebrate the seventy-fifth anniversary of the Irish Football Association. It was some days before an official message reached me through the post, to tell me I'd definitely been chosen. Naturally, I was quite pleased, but at the same time, I realized that I'd been a little lucky.

With the Wolves away in Moscow, their net being guarded by England's Bert Williams, and the Scottish F.A.'s extraordinary refusal to release any players from the Scottish League programme, the field was certainly narrowed. That was probably as well for me, since Bert Williams was playing very well indeed at that time, and must certainly have come into the reckoning, to say the least.

The full team was: myself; Sillett (England); McDonald (Scotland); Blanchflower (Ireland) (captain); Charles (Wales); Peacock (Ireland); Matthews (England); Johnstone (Scotland); Bentley (England); McIlroy (Ireland) and Liddell (Scotland). The only survivors of the British team which had trounced Europe 6-1 at Glasgow, eight years previously, were the two wingers, Stan Matthews and Billy Liddell.

Although I was naturally happy to be chosen – who wouldn't be – I felt disappointed when I read through the itinerary and saw that we were "on" no more than £25 and our expenses. It seemed a poor fee indeed for a match carrying such an imposing label; a match, what's more, which was a guaranteed sell-out for the Irish F.A. from the very day it was announced. After all, I got £50 for playing for Wales, and I felt that the fee should be at least as much, and logically, more.

In addition to Bert Williams, the Wolves had taken with them to Moscow the invaluable Billy Wright, captain of England, who would have been certain choice either at centre-half (thus releasing John Charles for centre-forward) or at wing-half.

Altogether, it wasn't a very representative British side. For one thing, I think that far too much attention was paid to giving every country a "fair" representation; three each from England, Scotland and Ireland, and two of us from Wales. Joe McDonald, the Sunderland left-back, had never played for his country, though the omission was quickly made up when the international season began.

On the other hand, the Europeans were very, very far from representing the full power of European football. How could they be said to do so when there wasn't a single Hungarian in the side, at a time when Hungary were still reckoned to be the World's best? Thus Puskas and Kocsis were not there to torment our defence from inside-forward, and Josef Boszik, the right-half and Member of Parliament, was also withdrawn by the Hungarian F.A.

Gerhard Hanappi, the famous blond Austrian, who was chosen for right-back, was in Australia at the time. Nothing, apparently, was heard from him at all, and it later transpired that he took this great representative game so lightly that he hadn't the least intention of being in Belfast, instead of Down Under. As for Bernard Vukas, who was called up at the last moment to play (and how he played!) at inside-left, he was on holiday at the seaside, at the time – and consequently, right out of training.

By a strange coincidence, Europe, too, fielded a player who had never represented his country. Odder still is the fact that he, unlike McDonald, hasn't been capped, yet. His name was Renzo Buffon, a fellow goalkeeper; a tall, dark, good looking young man who "kept" for Milan. The obvious choice for goal was Dynamos Lev Yachine but, I should mention, Europe were further handicapped by the fact that Russia would not play either, which meant no Yachine, no Netto and no Tatuchine, a fast outside-right who much impressed me when Spartak came to Highbury.

To return to Buffon, he had been for some years on the brink of the Italian national team, and I suppose this match will always rank as his greatest consolation. In his spare time he painted madonnas. I heard that, a couple of years previously, the selector of the Italian team had put his arm round Buffon, before one more in the series of matches for which he was reserve, and said, "My boy, I consider you to be my son."

"Papa!" Buffon promptly replied, "when am I going to play for Italy?"

Our team met at the Queen's Hotel, Manchester, and I travelled up with Tottenham's Danny Blanchflower, who was to skipper the side.

Danny is a very interesting character with whom to spend a train journey, especially if you like talking about football – or rather, listening. To get him going on the subject of soccer and soccer tactics means that you will probably never get a word in, so great is his knowledge of the game.

When we arrived at the Queen's Hotel, it was to be greeted by our team manager, Walter Winterbottom, and Jimmy McIlroy, Danny's compatriot, who exploits the very same dry brand of humour. Next came John Charles, who was to be my room-mate.

Our first training period together consisted of a match against Manchester City, at Maine Road and, considering that it was our first run-out together and that the league had not yet begun, I think we showed great promise. We beat the city 4-2, Jimmy McIlroy scoring three of our goals, and nippy little Bobby Johnstone the other. The following day, we were due to play Manchester United on the ground of Manchester University, but this was a meeting which very nearly did not take place at all.

The University ground, on which United were doing their pre-season training, was quite unknown to the driver of our coach, who was a comparative stranger to the Manchester area. Apparently there were a good many Mancunians who were no better off than he, for we were misdirected a number of times, and must have turned up at very nearly every sports ground in Manchester before we eventually found the right one.

The confusion did not seem to have affected our game, for we had another very good win; 5-2, this time, and it was Bobby Johnstone's turn to do the hat-trick. Perhaps I should point out that we were not playing the "Babes", as we were later to know and admire them. This was a United team which was only beginning to show the form of the great side it became. I myself only played in half of this match, for shortly before half-time I dived for a ball and succeeded in collecting a badly grazed elbow. Walter Winterbottom did not want to take any chances, and Bill Fraser, the Sunderland and Scotland goalkeeper, relieved me for the second half.

We were a pretty happy party, thanks not least to the Linfield trainer, Gerry Morgan, who seemed to have something amusing to say, whenever he opened his mouth. We flew to Belfast on the Wednesday before the match and trained on the

Ards ground, where we were well looked after by Sammy Smyth, the former Wolves star, then player-managing the Irish club.

Stanley Matthews trained, as always, quite on his own, in a corner of the field. Soccer lovers everywhere have marvelled at Stanley's soccer longevity, and the theory was often been put forward that he owes it to his methods of training. On this point, I am scarcely a qualified judge, for this was the only time I ever saw the Maestro in training, but I did take the opportunity to watch very carefully how he set about it.

He would start by doing a spell of lapping at a gentle pace, probably to get himself warmed up. Then followed a few loosening exercises, after which he would concentrate on sprinting in twenty-five yard bursts. Clearly this is the secret of his ability to beat any full-back in the world over that distance, with the ball at his feet. His training period would end, more often than not, with Stan kicking a ball around in a corner of the field, taking corner-kicks and practising centres. But don't ask me how he perfects and keeps in running order that fantastic swerve.

The day of the match was obviously more suited to the continentals than ourselves. They had had to make another late change to compensate for the absence of Hanappi. Julli Gustavsson, the big Swedish centre-half, who later went to make a fortune in Italy, was switched to right-back, thus letting the elegant Bob Jonquet of France play at centre-half. Thus the European team was:

Buffon (Italy); Gustavsson (Sweden); Von Brandt (Belgium); Ocwirk (Austria) (captain); Jonquet (France); Boskov (Yugoslavia); Soerensen (Denmark); Vukas (Yugoslavia); Kopa (France); Travassos (Portugal) and Vincent (France).

That may not have been the best side at Europe's disposal, but my word, it still looked pretty good; and so it proved to be.

We made a good start on the bone-hard Belfast pitch, but that is as much as one can say in our favour. After the teams had been introduced to Mr. Hanna, the Ulster Minister for Home Affairs, Danny Blanchflower won the toss against the giant Ocwirk, and little Raymond Kopa touched the ball off to begin a game that was going to spell the humiliation of British football. It did not take long before the continentals, in most un-continental fashion, gave me a shot to think about.

The ball came to Leschly Soerensen, the blond, veteran outside-right, who was meant to have retired from active Italian football. He dribbled beautifully, then put in such a shot that I really wish he had retired, for it took me all my time to smother it! Still, we fought back quickly, and Buffon went rocketing across the goal to put behind a shot from Roy Bentley, after Blanchflower had found him with a beautifully lobbed pass.

It wasn't long after that when Bernard Vukas gave me a taste of what to expect, later in the game. His beautiful ball control enabled him to dribble his mazy way through our defence as though he were waltzing at half-speed through some practice match – but there was nothing half-speed about the shot with which he capped his run. I had all my work cut out to get to it.

Our green-shirted team wasn't playing badly at all at this stage, however, and little Bobby Johnstone was showing bags of energy and initiative. He nearly got a goal with a lovely drive made from the left, but Buffon flew through the air again, got his hands to it, and Ocwirk cleared, just as wandering Roy Bentley was moving in to make sure.

Stanley Matthews came into the game in fits and starts, but the European right flank was working better than ours with

Soerensen, who set out in life as an inside-forward, dropping back cleverly to look for the ball. He beat me with one shot, but Joe McDonald, bless him, turned up on the goal line to squeeze the ball away.

Yet it was we who scored the first goal, after twenty-five minutes. Stanley Matthews gave it to Bobby Johnstone with a perfect centre, and Bobby ran on to the ball to hit it very hard past Buffon.

Within three minutes, Europe were level. A scramble in our goal mouth, a loose ball running out to Vincent, the French left-winger, and crack! it was home. The goal seemed to encourage Vincent. He tried hard for another one when he moved on to a cross ball by Soerensen and put in a bullet. I flung myself at it and managed to push it round the post for a corner. We were all square at half-time, but I didn't like the creamy fluency with which those polyglot European forwards were moving.

They began the second half like a whirlwind. Sturdy little Kopa, the roving French centre-forward, was popping up everywhere, most of all on the right-wing, and he gave Vincent a goal on a plate, practically under our bar, which his fellow countryman somehow managed to miss. Out came the ball to Vukas who put in a terrific shot (who says these continentals can't shoot....when they want to?). But luckily I was waiting for it, and the ball hurtled straight into my arms.

Europe's forwards were playing lovely, dominating football by now, well backed up by their wing-halves, Boskov and the mighty Ocwirk – yet they had to wait till thirteen minutes from time before they took the lead, and John Charles was primarily to be thanked for the delay. Then Vukas smashed one in from outside the penalty-area, and the score was 2-1.

There was plenty of work for me after that. Once I got the tips of my fingers to a shot from Kopa, which fortunately went over the bar. Then big John Charles popped up on the line to clear a shot from Vincent which had beaten me. Oh, dear, what a bombardment it was! Soerensen, who was roving all over the place, shot against the goal-post and I just contrived to fall on the ball, as it rebounded out into the six-yard area.

As a desperation measure, Danny Blanchflower moved John Charles up to centre-forward for the closing minutes, Danny himself playing centre-half. We were thoroughly well beaten by then, but this was really the last straw for our tormented defence, and it broke our camel's back. Vukas hit the post, then, three minutes from time, another twenty-yard screamer gave him his second goal. We'd had enough by now, but there was a last-minute twist of the knife in the wound. Bertie Peacock fouled Kopa in the box, and Vukas, who apparently told his captain, Ocwirk that he "didn't take penalties in Yugoslavia", made no bones about converting this one.

Great Britain 1, Europe 4, then, was the final tally, and we really could not put up the pale ghost of a complaint. We had been thoroughly bad – they were superlatively good.

After the match, both sides were presented plaques by officials of the Irish Football Association. In one corner were the badges of the four home soccer countries, while in the other there was a map of Europe. Peter Sillett, the big Chelsea back, was a little lucky not to lose his. We were invited to a Sportsmans' Club in Belfast, where I suddenly had the idea that it would be a good thing to write my name on the box of my plaque. Peter thought this was wise, and followed suit. On leaving the club, he totally forgot his plaque, and remembered nothing about it until we were on the aeroplane next morning, for London. All turned out well in the end, however, for some kind person found the box and posted it on to Peter, care of Chelsea.

Soerensen, a tall, fair-haired fellow, was with us at the club. He certainly had a thing or two to say about the game, and notably about his Great Britain equivalent, Stanley Matthews who, he was audacious enough to claim, "would not get into a continental team. I certainly wouldn't have him in my team. I admit he is a good ball player, but by overdoing his ball work he holds up the forward line by not passing the ball at the right time. Also, he very often gives a full-back a second chance to tackle him."

Of course, I could not agree with him. Even if Stan does give a back a second chance, the fact remains that he's always capable of beating him again. In my modest opinion, Stanley has always been a great winger, a great entertainer, and a player who has done wonderful things for British football.

Certainly he has his faults, and Soerensen has hit on one of them. I think he was right in saying that Stan might pass the ball a little more quickly. The few seconds he spends mesmerizing full-backs gives other defenders time to cover up. Another point worth making about his play is his knack of shielding the ball from an opponent. When Stan has the ball at his feet, there are not many players who can get near enough to him to take it away. Stan always plays with his arms held away from his body, so that a player coming in to tackle him has not only to get around his body, but round his arms, as well. Should they succeed in doing so, then Stanley has only to turn his body slightly for the poor defender to be back where he started. Some people might call this obstruction; I don't, because I consider that Stanley naturally plays this way. Len Shackleton of Sunderland was another fine ball player who played in almost similar style, although his arms used to move like pistons. At all events, there's nothing in the rules of football to say that you have to play with your arms pinned to your sides.

I want to end this chapter on what may seem an irrelevant note; with a word or two about a player who wasn't in that disastrous Belfast match, but deserved to be – Nat Lofthouse.

Why Nat did not get selected rather baffled me, for he is about the best centre-forward I have ever faced. He is always a great-hearted player, and a centre-half or goalkeeper playing against him could never enter the match thinking they were going to have an easy time of it. Nat is the type of player who, if he finds that the ball isn't coming to him, will go off looking for it, on his own account. He's always roaming dangerously into the open spaces, and takes up position with great intelligence.

Whenever he gets the ball near goal, be it in the air or on the ground, there's trouble in store for his opponents. He needs to have only a small area of the goal in his sights to let fly with great power and accuracy, either with his right foot or his left, and he certainly hits that ball hard. If a goalkeeper does manage to get to the ball, his fingers will tingle for a few minutes afterwards. I know from that painful and personal experience, for when I stopped one of his shots during a league match against Bolton Wanderers, I thought I had broken my wrist!

Nat's heading is phenomenally good, and it's rather an intriguing coincidence that he should have gone to the same Bolton school as that other great header of a football, Tommy Lawton. A Lofthouse header comes at you with a force which many forwards would like to be able to *shoot* with, and these headers are accurate, too. Furthermore, Nat never allows a goalkeeper to take a high cross without challenging him. Every time I play against Nat and go up for a high ball, I expect to have the pleasure of his company.

It was against Bolton and Nat that I played one of my most enjoyable games; a league match at Burnden Park, in 1956-57. The midfield play was very even, but Bolton had the edge on us in their shooting, so that I was given plenty of work. Fortunately, it was one of those days which occasionally fall to goalkeepers, when everything that they do is right. Most of my work consisted of dealing with shots by Nat from all angles – and with cutting out centres for which his sturdy figure was leaping.

With less than a minute to go, the score was 1-1, then Nat broke away. From fifteen yards, he let fly one of his rockets, and the ball travelled like a bullet for the top left-hand corner of the net. I went up in the appropriate direction, hoping but not really expecting to save. It's beaten me, I thought, but it hadn't. Somehow I got my right hand to it, and the ball flew round the post, to finish in the crowd behind the goal.

The spectators, knowing that the final whistle was due at any instant, hastily threw the ball back for the corner to be taken. Over came the kick, and it was one of those balls which are virtually marked "goalkeeper". I had taken all the other crosses in the match with ease – so why not this one? I moved out confidently to intercept, but I scarcely got off the goal line when a Bolton forward obstructed me, so that I remained totally earthbound. The ball went straight to the terrible feet of Nat Lofthouse, who promptly banged it home through a crowd of players.

We expected the referee to give us a free kick for blatant obstruction, but, to our amazement, he blew the final whistle instead, and the goal stood. We left the field with disappointment at being beaten so unkindly. Yet, at the same time, we knew we'd put up a good display. That, as someone may have remarked elsewhere, is football.

Walter Winterbottom chatting to the Great Britain players during a training spell in 1955. I wonder how many old favourites you can pick out?

Under floodlights at Moscow. I dive for the ball during the Arsenal match against the Dynamos. The result was Dynamo 5, Arsenal 0.

I fly through the air with the greatest of ease in order to prevent Viollet (Manchester United) getting there first: centre-half Fotheringham is in close attendance. Guy Fawkes Day 1955.

An anxious moment. With Spurs leading 2-0 I just managed to save what looked like a certain third goal. November 1957.

I am a great believer in weight lifting as a means of strengthening all the muscles of my body. Picture taken in the Arsenal gymnasium.

All the drama of soccer is in this picture, taken during an Arsenal v Chelsea match in December 1954. I am saving a penalty taken by Roy Bentley.

9
RED DRAGONS TRIUMPHANT

I missed my first real chance of playing at Wembley. It came in November 1954. Wales were due to meet England at the Empire Stadium, and I was then in the Welsh goal. Alas, Arsenal refused to release me from the previous night's match against Spartak. I was pretty upset by the decision, though I certainly came nowhere near to asking for a transfer. Derek Tapscott, however, did get his release for the game, which was just as well, for he had a wonderful match at outside-right. My own feeling was that I could have played in both games, and Welsh officials told me that I was probably right. But perhaps they decided that it would be wrong to risk my being injured against Spartak, and Wales having to take the field with a goalkeeper who had no previous practice with the team. At all events, the position went to Johnny King, of Swansea Town, and I watched the match, with much anxiety, from the stands.

I thought King did very well, especially as he had to face the trial of an international debut made at Wembley. He made his greatest save from Derek Tapscott, who had come back into defence. Derek took a flying kick at the ball, which skidded off his boot and flew for the goal like a bullet. King was ready though. With instinctive judgement, he hurled himself across and managed to punch the ball away.

England won 3-2 that day, but I thought they were lucky. It was one of those matches which raised the query, can a player get a hat-trick and still play badly? Roy Bentley scored all three of England's goals, the first hat-trick of his career, yet he had, on the whole, an unhappy ninety minutes.

Ivor Allchurch, Wales' blond inside-left, gave England's defence plenty of trouble that day. Generally, though,

I have not seen Ivor play for Wales as I know he can for Swansea. Off the field, you can't get a word out of him; he just sits down and thinks, speaking only when he is spoken to.

The following season, I had two of my most exciting matches for Wales. The first I am never in danger of forgetting, for we beat England; our first victory against them in the International Championship since 1938. The game was played in the fever-heat of Ninian Park, and I seemed to be diving at feet all the time, and mostly at the feet of Wolverhampton's Dennis Wilshaw. Dennis is a poacher, the sort of player with whom you have to be on your toes, all the time, for he is always hanging around the goal, looking for chances.

Once, in this tremendous Cardiff battle, he tried to fool me with a back-heel flick instead of a first-time shot – and he very nearly succeeded. The ball was going away from me, but I managed to put out a finger, and turn it over the bar, which it struck on its way. With Nat Lofthouse lining up beside him, it was anything at all but a goalkeeper's benefit.

I remember how good we felt before that game, we Welsh players. We were all singing away in the dressing-room, relaxed and encouraged, perhaps, by the Ninian Park atmosphere. It was, to coin a phrase, electric, and its electricity was all working for us.

Derek Tapscott was in splendid form against Roger Byrne – he always seemed to play well when he met Roger, and I believe the explanation may be found in the previous year's game at Wembley. Derek did just what he liked that afternoon, and everything seemed to come off. He was flicking balls over his shoulder with his heel and catching them on his instep, just like Len Shackleton at his greatest. The memory lingered with Roger.

It was Derek who scored our first goal, after thirty-eight minutes. Noel Kinsey through-passed down the middle, and

Derek was after it like a flash. It looked as if Billy Wright or Roger Byrne would get hold of it first, but Derek was too quick for them. He was on the ball, to belt it into the roof of the net, and caper with joy like a prancing stallion.

In a couple of minutes, we had scored again. Roy Paul took the ball down the right – though he was playing at left-half. Up in the air went Cliff Jones to head home his centre – and England's solitary reply came from big John Charles, who headed the ball past me, six minutes after half-time.

I was kept very busy after that. Even Stanley Matthews came swerving his way into the middle, and twice gave me stinging drives to hold. A quarter of an hour from time, I had one hell of a save to make from Don Revie; a first-time drive from sixteen yards, just inside the upright. I threw myself full length to touch it away. I should have held the ball, I know, but the sheer force of the drive took it through my hands. And we held out to win.

There was one feature of this match which did not please me, and that was the charging used by one or two of our forwards on England's goalkeeper, Bert Williams. Trevor Ford, in particular, have him no peace, and though charging the goalkeeper is legal enough, I thought it was overdone here. It doesn't get you anywhere and it won't, except in very exceptional circumstances, bring you any goals. The only thing it might do is play a part in preventing goals, by forcing the goalkeeper to clear hastily, instead of putting the ball to a colleague. This, in my view, is the reason why goalkeepers should definitely be chargeable. Over on the Continent, the unwritten no charging rule allows them to do just as they like.

I was certainly lucky with the Press I had after this England game. One Sunday paper headed its report, KELSEY THE MAGNIFICENT. "Well done Wales!" it said. "You deserved this Soccer triumph." I thought so, too.

Our next date was against Scotland, in mid-week, at Hampden. Perhaps it was the missing Ninian Park atmosphere, but we showed none of the same pep in the dressing-room, before the match. "Why aren't you singing now?" asked one of the selectors. I suppose it's because Hampden was not Cardiff.

It had already been a hectic week for three of our side, John Charles, Derek Tapscott and myself. Leeds United had fixed a home friendly against Arsenal for the Monday, and, somewhat expectedly, they wanted John to play. Leeds without John, after all, was rather like London without the Tower. For the same reason, Arsenal called on Derek Tapscott and myself, which meant that the Hampden game was our second within three days. The unfortunate thing was that the only train which would take us to Glasgow left at two in the morning, so there was no question of going to bed. The three of us sat up in the hotel, playing cards with Dennis Evans, until it was time to leave. We did have sleepers, but I, for one, can never sleep in them. We arrived in Glasgow at eight o'clock, and the only training we had time for was a few sprints on the Wednesday morning, for we spent all Tuesday resting. I rather felt it was a little unfair. We should have been released from that friendly, especially as Wales, after our victory against England, definitely stood a chance of landing the International Championship.

That chance went in Hampden's November afternoon. I didn't think much of the so-called Hampden Roar, perhaps because the stadium wasn't anywhere near full. As for the pitch, it was in poor condition, very rough and bumpy. From the stand, it looks just like Wembley, but that impression doesn't survive very long, once you find yourself treading it. I was very disappointed.

On the other hand, Hampden's general facilities are superb. We were shown round them beforehand and for me, of course, it was my first sight of the famous stadium. There's a fine Press Box, though, like Wembley's, it is a bit high, a place from which photographs may be radioed from the ground, and a fascinating trophy room, with photographs of matches, banners and souvenirs, presented to Queens Park, the owners. So huge are the stands, so many the rooms and corridors, that I could easily imagine myself getting lost in there.

As for the match, it was another occasion when I seemed to be down among people's feet, alternating this with leaping to take crosses. It was made harder by the fact that I was hobbling for most of the game, after Lawrie Reilly had opened the score for Scotland – or would have done, had not referee Reg Leafe given him offside. His header beat me, and we collided, his knee catching me on the thigh. I was limping for the rest of that disconcertingly busy game, most of which was dominated by Scotland. Bobby Johnstone, Reilly's former team-mate at Hibs, was in particularly good form, and he scored both Scotland's goals, with a couple of crackers – one in each half.

Reilly's goal might well have been a good one, too. It was given offside, but there wasn't a lot in it, for the ball came over at a funny angle. I also remember a save I made from Jackie Henderson of Portsmouth, who was on the wing for Scotland that afternoon. I was beaten by a cross, but before Jackie could take advantage of the fact, I managed to recover, get my arms round him, and hold the ball.

It was a useful Scottish team, with little Bobby Johnstone playing very skilfully and dangerously, chiming in beautifully with wee Reilly. Other players who took my eye were Bobby Evans, the red-haired Celtic half-back, playing cultured football with his jersey outside his shorts, George Young and Tommy Younger. George, the massive, dominating Rangers centre-half, has been called the Rock of Gibraltar, and you could easily see why, that afternoon. His heading of the ball was unerring, and he even came up the field once to give me a shot to hold. He had little difficulty in taking care of our inside-forward trio; indeed, I don't quite know what went wrong with us, that day. The spirit we'd shown against England just seemed, somehow, to be lacking.

Big, blond Tommy Younger was my opposite number in the Scottish goal, and very good he looked. Not that he was bothered unduly, but I've had opportunities since then of appreciating his very considerable merits. There's nothing showy about his play, and he always seems to be immensely solid. His positioning is so intelligent that he seems to be there on the spot every time, while he is such a large fellow that it takes quite a bit of effort to bundle the ball out of his arms.

Anyway, it wasn't our day. I had to pull out a rather desperate leap, in the second half, to save a cracker from the Scottish right-back, of all people – Alex Parker, of Falkirk.

Meanwhile, what was happening at Highbury? Our team had been changing quite a bit, and there were a number of new faces. One of them belonged, I was happy to see, to my old pal Len Wills, who made the right-back position his own about this time. He came in for his first league match in the North London derby against the Spurs, in 1954, at White Hart Lane. Both our regular backs were missing, and it must have been quite a trial for Len. Nor was he much encouraged when one of our directors, who'd better stay anonymous, visited the dressing-room before the game and remarked to Tom Whittaker in a stage whisper, "Who's that?"

"Len Wills," said Tom.

"Well, have we signed him? Is he an amateur?"

"Poor Len. He heard every word of this, but he did not allow it to upset him. He went out to play a fine game, and we had a brilliant win that afternoon. I rate Len as a very thoughtful and very constructive player. A section of the crowd at Highbury (those unfortunate sections!) seems to think that he takes things too casually, but they could not be more wrong. This is just Len's way of playing. He won't be rushed, and shouting at him is going to make no difference at all. Such people seem to think that if Len and the winger meet on the half-way line, Len should jump in and tackle him. That is not the way we play at Highbury.

Off the field, Len is very interested in watch repairing. Whenever we are touring abroad, and one of the boys wants to but a watch, then Len is always brought along to pass expert judgement. If the verdict is "no", then the watch will never be bought.

Our cup luck at Highbury was rather mixed about this time. We had a good 5-1 home win against Aston Villa in the third round of 1954 – but then we had not expected too much trouble, after being three up against them in a league match the previous Saturday, after only fourteen minutes. That match was unhappily abandoned. Actually, they gave us a great deal more trouble in the cup tie than the score suggests, and kept me pretty active. I was rather on form that day, and, despite all Arsenal's goals, the Press seemed to think that I had something to do with our win, as well. At any rate, I recall picking up the *Sunday Pictorial* to read, somewhat to my surprise, KELSEY ACES VILLA.

Next came Norwich City, at Highbury, and we didn't like the draw at all. Far from being happy and confident when drawn against a Third Division side, we are always afraid of playing them. They throw everything at you, and you never get time to move the ball, whereas First Division footballers will jockey you. We find that the Third Division boys, like the poor, are always with us.

As you may remember, we lost that Norwich game, although the early signs were all in our favour. Norwich, for instance, were awarded a penalty, and I followed my usual practice by coming out of goal to bet Ireland's Bobby Brennan that he would not score. Nor did he. He seemed to stab the ground with his foot, and the ball just bobbled along the ground, no trouble at all to pick up. "That's a good let-off," I thought to myself, "now we can set about them." But I was too confident, too soon.

The next major event came when both Brennan and Alex Forbes were sent off. The incident rather surprised me. The two of them got into a hard tackle, and both of them became a bit annoyed. However, no blows were struck, and it was something of a shock when the referee banished them both to the dressing-rooms. It was a bit hard, I thought, especially in a cup match, where this sort of thing tends to create bad feeling before you start. Later, at the inquiry into the incident, Forbes was vindicated.

Although we lost, and although, Norwich played very gallantly, I don't think we were flattered, on the run of play. Tommy Johnston, the blond centre-forward who later scored so many good goals for Leyton Orient, scored twice for the Canaries, with that formidably dangerous head of his. I think I might have had the first one, if the ball had not grazed Bill Dodgin's head, just as I had picked my spot. The second was one of those headers you can do very little about. The ball was crossed from the right and Johnston, meeting it some ten yards out, flicked it beautifully, so that it went in off the upright.

In the last ten minutes, it was the tall Ken Oxford who saved Norwich. I don't believe that I even touched the ball, during the final quarter of an hour, except to gather the occasional over-kick or cautious back-pass. At the end of the match, Bill Lewis, the Norwich left-back, collapsed on to

Arthur Milton, and had to be helped off. Logie's scrambled goal, glided in through a bunch of players, pulled back the leeway, but was not enough to save us. It was a real blow, just as it was a real triumph for Norwich. I heard that the party they held on the train, on the way home, cost them £78!

Bill Dodgin was having his first full season in Arsenal's side, at centre-half. He had joined us from Fulham, where the crowd had given a rough time both to him and Bill senior, his father, and the club's manager. It's strange how many players seem to start very well with their new club, then go back for a while, as though the impetus had somehow petered out. This was the case with "Young Bill". There was a period, after his excellent beginning, when he didn't quite know when to go for the man, and when to stay out, though his height saw to it that he was rarely beaten "upstairs". Later on, that spell of indecision became no more than a memory, and he settled down to become an able, "safety first" type of centre-half, who will clear first time for preference, his chief concern that the defence gets out of trouble.

Bill is a most intelligent fellow, serious in his approach to the game and to life in general, but quite a humorist as well. He never loses a chance to study football, and enjoys his busman's holidays, as I do myself. Once, at a mid-week match in which Arsenal were not involved, I remember that I met a certain film producer whom I knew.

"Why are *you* here?" the producer asked.

"Well," I said, "you go to the pictures...."

When the blackboard comes out at Highbury, Bill's always pointing out what should be done. Outside soccer, his chief hobby is gramophone records, and he has a collection of four or five hundred or all types, though I believe he is specially partial to jazz and blues.

For a spell, our centre-half was Bill Dickson, the Irish international who joined us from Chelsea. Where Bill Dodgin is a reserved sort of person, Bill Dickson was frequently laughing and joking – until he suddenly became dead serious. Until you got to know him well, this could be rather bewildering. I thought he was a darned good centre-half to play behind, and I was sorry – with no disrespect to Bill – to see him go, a prey to recurrent injuries. When he got the ball he always used it, and although he was not very tall, he could get up very well to the crosses; there were few centre-halves indeed who could beat him in the air.

But oh, those accidents and injuries! If there were any injuries going, then Bill had them: shoulders dislocated, slipped discs, cartilages, the whole lot. He came back to the team at the beginning of the 1955-6 season, when we all hoped he would be fit. But in the opening stages of the game at Blackpool with which we kicked off our league programme, he fell to the ground, clutching his shoulder; and that, effectively, was that.

I have been talking of cup ties, and must devote a few words to the way Wolves put us out in 1955, after a very late goal by Tom Lawton had squeezed us through against Cardiff. I, for one, had been all set for a replay, virtually on my "doorstep".

The one goal of the Molineux game was anticlimax. Dennis Wilshaw came through with the ball, from about six yards out, and shot past me. But just as the crowd were getting ready to congratulate one another, Dennis Evans made a fantastic save, flicking the ball over the bar with his head, and some four feet off the ground. We were all delighted at this escape, and thought it would probably be the turning point. Perhaps we were too delighted, for Walley Barnes, instead of taking up the customary corner-kick position, just inside the goal-post, was standing six or seven yards out. The corner came over rather low, and Royston Swinbourne dashed in to kick it home, just inside the upright where Walley would normally have been standing. "You were a bit slap-happy after Dennis's save," Tom Whittaker told us, afterwards, and it was hard to disagree with him.

Tom Lawton, scorer of our goal against Cardiff, was rather a surprising buy by the Arsenal, for he was right at the end of his famous career, when we – perhaps I should say they signed him from Brentford. He wasn't, perhaps, the perfect fit at Highbury. I remember him telling Cliff Holton how important the neck muscles were, for heading.

"When I was younger," he said, "I'd go like this," and showed Cliff a sharp forward jerk of the head.

Next morning, when Cliff turned up for training, he gave us all an unorthodox greeting. "Good morning" – a sharp jerk of the head – "Good morning," another jerk, "Good morning."

Tommy, of course, was a superb header of a football, and he certainly took it very seriously. Heading, indeed, sometimes seemed for him a cross between a science and a religion. When we were coming back in the car from a match at Preston, I remember him saying to Tom Whittaker, with great seriousness, "I don't know....I should have put bottom spin on that header, but I put on top spin. So it came off the goalkeeper's fists and went over the bar, instead of into the goal." Tom was afterwards a little sceptical.

Meanwhile, if the personnel was changing a bit at Highbury, the practical joking remained unaltered. On a couple of occasions, Dennis Evans was the victim. Once, some of the boys found in a Birmingham paper – we were up there for a match – an entry form for a cycle race. They filled it in with Dennis's name, care of the Arsenal Stadium, which brought a telephone call for the surprised Dennis, when he reported for training next Monday, asking him if he would confirm his "entry".

On another occasion, Joe Wade, back at the old telephone, rang up Dennis's wife in the guise of an official of the Metropolitan Water Board. "I'm so sorry," he said, "but we're having to cut off the water. Will you please fill up all the baths, buckets, pots and pans in the house, because the water won't be on again till six o'clock.

Iris Evans complied, and when Dennis walked in later in the day, it was to find water, water everywhere. It did not take him a moment to realize that Wadey had chalked up another victim.

Talking of Birmingham, and practical jokes which were hatched there, another one was played on our winger, Mike Tiddy. I rang him up from my hotel room, telling him I was a sports reporter of one of the Birmingham newspapers; we wanted him to write us an article, "on your rise from Cornish village football to playing for the Arsenal".

"Certainly," said Mike.

"And mention the Trevor Ford book," I told him, "the one that has just come out. Nothing nasty, of course."

"Certainly," said Mike.

"There's a five-pound cheque in the post," I went on. "You should get it next week, when you go back to London."

So up went Mike to his room, ready for composition, eager to turn out the 500 words which would earn him a fiver. He was sharing a room with Cliff Holton, and when Cliff saw him writing he said, "Come on, Mike, let's have the light out. There's a match tomorrow and I want to sleep."

Poor Mike finished his article by the light of the corridor, and left it downstairs with the porter, as I'd asked, but naturally it was myself who picked it up and read it. The sequel was a little unhappy, for Mike spent his match bonus on the strength of the fiver that never was.

Mike's appearances in the first team, since he joined us from Cardiff City with Gordon Nutt, have tended to be spasmodic, but Dennis Evans, of course, settled down to become captain. He's a strong thoughtful player, and it takes a good winger to get by him. He's fairly fast, too, especially when you consider that he broke a leg, during his army days. Though the leg bends in where it should bend out, there do not seem to have been any real ill-effects.

At the time I am writing this Dennis is a useful captain, though he doesn't drive the side as Joe Mercer used to do. He is a very friendly soul, but forceful, too. If five fellows were in a conversation, you'd know very well if Dennis was among them – which is fair enough, for a captain.

Left-half David Bowen is a good captain, too – of Wales. But since he lives and trains at Northampton, perhaps it is not surprising that Dennis gets the vote from most of the boys. It is a bit of a disadvantage to have to tell Dave the form on the Saturday of the match, after the rest of us have actually been trying and thrashing it out during the week.

I've a good deal of admiration for Dave, both as a player and skipper. When he became captain of Wales, I thought he played better than when he had no responsibilities; his slightly bow legs, his clenched fists, driving the team on, would make him reminiscent of Mercer, even if he did not fill the same position on the field. For me, he is one of the best wing-halves playing today, and I would not like to name any better in Britain. He's a strong tackler who uses the ball well, though I'd say he was inclined to play better with the direct type of winger. With little Joe Haverty, there have been times when short-passing has been exaggerated. I prefer him when he plays for Wales, behind the straightforward, speedy Cliff Jones. Dave pushes the ball through, and Cliff does the rest.

Off the field, he is a friendly sort of fellow. He owns a small-holding in Northampton, with 250 chickens, so there's plenty for him to do, during the week. He's also studying to be a physiotherapist.

Early in 1956, it seemed there were going to be major changes in the set-up at Highbury. Alec Stock, the manager of Leyton Orient, was appointed assistant manager to Tom Whittaker, though (what's in a name or a title?) Jack Crayston remained assistant manager, too.

Stock travelled with the team to Villa Park, presumably to get the feel of things. I had not met him, and in the dressing-room before the match, I asked our chief scout, Joe Shaw, "Aren't you going to introduce me to Alec Stock?"

"It'll take place on Monday," said Joe, "when he's officially introduced." This was protocol indeed. And when the introduction came, what a calamitous business it was.

"Right," said Alec, young and very brisk, "we'll go up in the gym and have a natter." The "nattering" was done by him, forcefully.

We were stunned, all of us. We just were not used to being spoken to in this way. Tom Whittaker was a father to us. Doubtless Stock had been authorised to speak as he had, but no wonder there were some long faces, afterwards.

Alec's next move was to introduce group training, where previously it had been individual. Group training certainly has its advantages, though what's sauce for the goose is not necessarily sauce for the gander, so far as football is concerned, and it certainly does not suit everybody. A heavy man like Stan Charlton might need twenty laps, where a footballer of Bill Dodgin's physique needs less.

Under the new regime, we sprinted between posts, chasing footballs, turned sharply, and came back the other way. That was good exercise, as were other ideas of Alec's, but personally I did not much like his way of putting them over.

One of his new rules was that there was to be no smoking anywhere near the ground. Now, excessive smoking obviously has no place in a soccer player's life, but I, for one, like my occasional cigarette a lot, and was a little resentful.

With one of two exceptions – notably Stan Charlton, who had been with Stock at Orient, and thought he was great – nobody seemed to me to enjoy the new methods. The trouble was that nobody had the nerve to tell him so; if they had, it might have been very different. But it was a question of people boxing clever, in the belief that Alec had been brought in, a young man and a new broom, to be the next manager.

Of course, Alex Stock did not stay at Highbury. As everyone knows, he went back to Orient, the newspaper announcement preceding his actual decision.

I can't say that his departure was unanimously regretted, but it would be unfair not to admit that he did some good, as well. Our training has remained more strict, ever since his spell.

10
THE PASSING OF TOM WHITTAKER

The death of Tom Whittaker, shocking in itself, was all the more painful to us Arsenal players because of its surprise. We all knew Tom had been very ill, of course, and knew that he had been confined to bed throughout the summer. But on that October day in 1956 when I arrived at the Arsenal Stadium for training, the story was that Tom was on his way back, had recovered splendidly; that he had gone to the south coast, to tone himself up, before making his return to Highbury.

Nothing, at first glance, seemed different about the Arsenal Stadium, that morning. Then somebody, I forget who, said to me, "The Governor passed away during the night." The affect of the news was to stun me. I couldn't believe it; after all, wasn't he supposed to be so much better and stronger, now. But it was only true, alas. He had died in hospital, had never gone to the south coast, at all. This had merely been a story put out by Highbury in an attempt to protect Tom from Press inquiries.

The shock was such that we just couldn't talk about it. And just as Tom Whittaker, then the trainer, had apparently been the most grieved of all when Herbert Chapman died, so Billy Milne, our present trainer, was the saddest among us, now. He and Tom had been like two brothers; they had worked together at Highbury for over thirty years, from their playing days. Poor Billy was choked by the death of his friend. He's as tough as nails, a hero of the First World War, and yet, for that next week, he'll forgive me if I say that he suddenly and temporarily seemed to go as soft as jelly. He could not hear the Governor's name mentioned, without tears coming to his eyes. And there were tears in my own at the funeral, where Cliff

Holton, as skipper, and I, as next senior professional, were token bearers, at the request of Mrs Whittaker.

Tom had been a wonderful bulwark at Highbury, a great trainer, a loyal player, a fine manager. He had seen the Arsenal rise from an obscure team, struggling for its place in the First Division, to one which is held to have failed if it isn't in the running for Cup or League. To us players, he had been a friend and even a father.

Perhaps it was because we were so upset that we were soundly beaten at Everton, in our next match. We played as though we had our tails between our legs, black bands round our arms, and lost by four goals to nil. There was a two minutes silence before the match, in commemoration of the Governor, and a speech of tribute by the Everton chairman.

We all hoped that Jack Crayston would be the next manager, and we expected it, too. After all, as assistant manager, we reckoned that it was his duty and prerogative to step up. He had been with the club since 1934, when he joined them as a right-half from Bradford. I'd liked the way he handled things when I was in the reserves, as I've mentioned before, even if he was *too* much of a gentleman, at times.

For my own part, I had another reason for hoping the choice would fall on Jack – I was afraid that Alec Stock might return. And if he had, I'd made no secret of my intention to ask for a transfer.

When Jack was, in fact, appointed, we players were very pleased. And he did very well, too, in his first season. When he took over, the team was having rather a bad time of it. But he took us to fifth position in the league and the sixth round of the cup, in which we were knocked out by a blatantly offside goal.

Since Tom Whittaker's death, the greatest difference at Highbury is that we no longer go upstairs with a grouse, as we always used to. It's all done, now, in the room between the two dressing-rooms – for sentimental motives. Indeed, the Governor's office is unused throughout the week. Only Sir Bracewell Smith, the chairman, occupies it on Saturdays when we are playing at home.

When I said that Billy Milne was most touched by the Governor's death, I should have linked his name with that of Miss Grover, the Governor's devoted and immensely efficient secretary. One couldn't have done without the other, and I sometimes used to wonder which was the manager. Miss Grover had been at Highbury since pre-war days, and she could lay her hands on any document or record within a matter of seconds.

It would be useless to deny that with the death of Tom Whittaker, the Chapman Era proper came to an end at Highbury. But the tradition itself did not die, for there were men like Billy Milne, Jack Crayston and assistant secretary Bob Wall to carry it on into the future.

In May, 1958, Jack Crayston resigned as manager.

11
WELSH WEMBLEY – AND A WORLD CUP EXIT

My first appearance at Wembley Stadium, in goal, lasted exactly thirteen minutes. It was at this moment that Johnny Haynes put one of his clever through passes down the centre, and Tom Finney chased it. I had to make a hurried dash out of the Welsh goal to reach the ball before him, and this I succeeded in doing. But Tom was bearing down on me so fast that he found it impossible to check his pace.

I was in a kneeling position when he collided with me, and his knee went into my back. There was an instant of severe pain, and I had immediate visions of a similar injury to the one I had suffered against the Wolves, in my fourth league game. Going off on a stretcher, my thoughts were rather mixed. First, I thought about the injury, wondering with anxiety whether anything had gone wrong internally. Then I tried to imagine the feelings of my wife, who was up there in the stand, watching me – and those of my mother, who was looking at the game on television. Father had come up for the match, and, after all, he was used to seeing goalkeepers in the wars.

Arriving in the dressing-rooms, we found the stadium doctor there, waiting for me. He had a look at my back, found the skin was broken, and gave me an injection on the spot. Presumably this was a precaution against gangrene, for the football world still has not forgotten the sad fate of Sheffield Wednesday's young Derek Dooley, the centre-forward who lost a leg, after an injury at Preston.

My injury was not only a personal blow; it was also a tragedy for Wales, who were actually leading at the time. John Charles had scored the goal, one of his best, and a goal worthy of the Empire Stadium. Ivor Allchurch had taken a free kick on our right flank, just outside England's penalty-area. The ball sailed over the goal mouth and Big John, outleaping all the England defenders, headed the ball firmly past Ditchburn's left hand into the far side of the net.

How pleased our team manager, Manchester United's Jimmy Murphy, must have felt at that moment – and how depressed he must suddenly have been, when I was injured, only minutes later. Jimmy is a very forceful character, who is doing great things for Welsh football, without having any luck at all. Almost every Welsh eleven of which he has been in charge has had its team plans dashed, either by injuries during the match, or by last-minute changes. I am sure that when the ball starts to run a little more kindly for him, he will bind the team into the old fighting force that it used to be: and then England, Scotland and Ireland can look out.

We'd gone to the Empire Stadium full of confidence, having worked out various useful plans at the Vickers Sports Ground, in Weybridge. Jimmy talked tactics all through the coach journey, reminding us time and again that on their two previous visits to Wembley, Wales had been beaten 3-2 and 5-2; he did not want to see an English hat-trick. When we got there, he took us straight out on the pitch, threw a ball among us, and said, "Go on, lads, get used to the turf. You'll find it very tiring." By this point, I had just about got over the attack of butterflies which had been afflicting me, at the prospect of my first Wembley. Alan Harrington, the young Cardiff City half-back, also playing his first Wembley, was a fellow sufferer.

We lost the game, of course, and it looked a pretty good argument for substitute goalkeepers. During the following summer, the British Association turned the idea down on the grounds that it would be unfair to a team which lost a man who wasn't a goalkeeper, playing against a side whose goalkeeper had been substituted. But surely such cases are very rare. In the meantime, many a potentially good match will no doubt continue to be ruined, for it needs a recognized goalkeeper to take over this, the most specialized of all soccer positions.

Alf Sherwood went in goal and played bravely enough, but Wales were hit again when Mel Charles became another stretcher case, being carried into the dressing-rooms after he had taken a hard drive from Johnny Haynes full in the stomach. Fortunately he had recovered in time to come out for the second half, and I tried to join him. It was my intention to shadow Stanley Matthews wherever he went, but this proved to be quite impossible; the pain in my side was so intense that I could hardly run. I am sure that even if Stan had slowed himself down to walking pace, I still could not have kept up with him.

England recovered, and won the match 3-1. Afterwards, I felt that Alf had done well enough in goal, and made him a present of my jersey.

Ivor Allchurch emerged from his usual silence to have the last, telling word on the game. When Jeff Hall, the England right-back, commented, "It's always difficult playing against ten men," Ivor replied, "Try playing ten men against eleven – that's really difficult."

At the end of the 1956-7 season, Wales began their qualifying programme in the World Cup. Alas, we didn't manage it and the chance of a trip to Sweden was lost. But there was some interesting football and some interesting travelling involved, and we did not miss by very much. Since the British International Championship was no longer recognized as an automatic qualifying group for the top two teams, Wales were included in a group with East Germany and Czechoslovakia, two Iron Curtain countries.

We beat the Czechs at Cardiff, though it was a pretty close thing. Indeed, having read about their reputation in the

Press, we scarcely expected to beat them at all. They had been compared with the Hungarians, and we knew what that meant. Deep down inside us, I think that most of us Welsh players believed that we, like England against the Hungarians, were in for a hiding. On the other hand, we did like the fact that the Press had made the Czechs hot favourites to beat us. At least we could go into the game with everything to gain and nothing to lose; though as it turned out, the comparison between the Czechs and that magnificent Hungarian side was rather ill-informed. They were good, certainly – but by no means as good as that.

Three days before the game, we met at our H.Q., the Angel Hotel, Cardiff. John Charles arrived there from Italy, the envy of us all, for he had been the subject of the famous deal between Juventus and Leeds United, which would leave him £10,000 the richer. He was accompanied by Iso Cohen, one of the Juventus directors, and the club's agent, the tubby, voluble, energetic little Calabrian, Gigi Peronace, who spoke English well.

He had been to look over living accommodation in Turin. When he arrived at the hotel, I remember the he perched on the edge of my chair, pulled out a fag-end, and lit it.

"Ten thousand pounds," I said, "and you're still smoking dog-ends?"

"You mustn't waste them," John answered, seriously.

"What kind of place are they giving you, John? asked his younger brother, Mel, also in the Welsh team.

"Marvellous," John said. "It's a villa on the side of a hill, and they've slung in a spaghetti orchard."

"Lucky devil," said Mel, and we thought that he had fallen for it. But later that year, before our return match against East Germany, we learned differently.

"I see John's doing well with Juventus," he said.

"Has he sent you any spaghetti?" someone asked.

"No," said Mel, with a straight face. "It isn't ripe yet; they haven't picked it."

For the first game with the Czechs, we did our pre-match training at our usual place, the Guest, Keen, Nettlefolds Sports Ground, though the Czechs were surprisingly allowed to train at Ninian Park itself. Cardiff City's Welsh League ground was made available to us, but we turned down the offer.

The Czechs began that game with some smooth, attacking football, but their movements came to a dead end when they reached the eighteen-yard line; and when they did break through, they found John Charles at his best. Certainly they were living up to their big reputation as far as mid-field football was concerned, but we knew that it needs a little more than that to get goals, and results. Indeed, the only goal of that first half, and, as it turned out, of the match, was scored by Wales. Cliff Jones made ground on the left, then pushed the ball through to Derek Tapscott, who was unmarked. His long cross beyond the far post was headed back into the goal mouth by Terry Medwin, and young Roy Vernon of Blackburn Rovers came racing in to smash home a great, right-footed, first-time shot.

The second half went much the way of the first. The Czechs often looked as though they might break through, but John Charles, playing the game of his life, was there to prevent them from reaching me. Until the last ten minutes of the match, I think that all I did was to gather a few crosses, and collect the handful of loose balls that came my way.

Midway through the half, Charles came out of a tackle, fell to the ground, and started to roll over, clutching his leg, obviously in great pain. My wife, who was sitting near Gigi Peronace in the grandstand, tells me that the little Italian was up on his feet, crying frantically, "Oh, my Johnny! What's happened to you, my Johnny?" Later, he told us that he feared the worst – a broken leg, which would cost Juventus John's services. In the circumstances, I think it was generous of the Italian club to allow John to make the summer continental tour with Wales.

In the eightieth minute, the Czechs somehow and suddenly found a way past John, who was now back on his feet; his trouble had been nothing worse than cramp, thank goodness. The trouble started when Moravicka, the Czech inside-forward, shot from inside the penalty-area. The ball hit my right-hand post, ran along the goal-line, and just missed hitting the left-hand post, as well. Pazdera, the outside-right, came running in after the loose ball, which I just managed to reach before him.

That near thing seemed to put new life into the Czechs. They really turned on the heat, and I must have made at least ten saves during those closing minutes, one of which I shall always remember. Kraus put in a terrific shot which came straight at me. It was a bit too hot for me to hold, and the ball hit my chest, spun up over my shoulder, and started dropping dangerously near the goal-line. I turned round, stopped the ball with one hand, and held it stationary, long enough to show the linesman that it had not gone over the line. Then I cleared it, to the accompaniment of great laughter from the crowd. I suppose it probably seemed a cheeky thing for me to do, at that stage of the game.

In the closing seconds, the Czechs again came within an ace of getting the equalizer. This time it was Svoboda who put in a great shot (they'd found those shooting boots somewhere) that made me stretch to my top left-hand corner. Somehow I got a hand to the ball, and turned it over the bar. Before the corner could be taken, the referee had blown his whistle for time; and, against all the odds, Wales had won. The crowd surged on to the field to mob us, and the fight we had to get through them was harder than the fight we had to win the match.

It looked, then, as though we had a pretty good chance of eventually getting through to Sweden. True, we had had some luck against the Czechs, but we could take a fairly useful side to the Continent for our two away qualifying games. Big John was going, and we had some dangerous forwards, especially young Cliff Jones, Swansea's outside-left.

What speed that boy has! I have always thought the Arsenal's Danny Clapton was one of the fastest forwards in the game, but Cliff runs like a rabbit; he can keep going for a thousand yards, let alone twenty. He has lovely ball control, too. When we drew with Scotland at Hampden, in November 1957, I remember him going diagonally across the field to Scotland's right-hand corner flag in a straight line, beating five players on the way with body-swerve. He didn't beat them in tackles for the ball; he just "sent" them.

Cliff's one fault is that he keeps going....and going....and going. If only he could slip the ball inside... He's very lightly built of course, and has next to no weight to carry, which must help him to move as fast as he does. What's more, he could do it on army training, playing as many as three matches a week!

Off the field he's another Quiet Man, and one rarely heard a word from him, though when one does, it's often drily humorous. He's always pulling another Swansea player, burly Mel Charles, to pieces. Mel insists on regarding him as a little boy, and Cliff plays up to it. "Yes," he says, "all right then – Dad." He's the finest left-winger in Britain, for my money, and we probably haven't seen the best of him yet.

Our first continental match, that May, was in Leipzig, against the East Germans – rather an unknown quantity. We flew from London to Berlin, via Hamburg, and there took a coach for Leipzig, for what must be one of the dreariest journeys in the world. Oh, how tired we got on that *autobahn*, which, seemed to run right through the middle of nowhere. Very rarely indeed did we see a building; as for people, we could not have passed more than four or five of them throughout the whole trip. Even the traffic was very light, considering this was, after all, the main road between two of the largest cities in Eastern Germany; most of it consisted of Russian Army vehicles.

In Leipzig, we stayed at the state-controlled Astoria Hotel. When we got there, there was rather a nice touch by our hosts: waiting for each of us were five stamped postcards. Our training was to be done on the small ground of a local club. It attracted plenty of onlookers, who took a great interest in everything we did.

The day before the match, we had our first look at the so-called Hundred Thousand Stadium, where it was to be played; and we were impressed. The stadium, a great bowl without any cover, derives its name from the fact that it can hold 100,000 spectators, all seated, plus another 10,000 standing at the top of the terracing. But these unfortunates are so high up that they must surely have needed binoculars, to make out what was going on down on the field of play. The stadium is surrounded by sports facilities of every description; tennis and netball courts, training grounds and a huge swimming-pool. Remarkably enough, the people of Leipzig built it with voluntary labour, out of bomb debris – and the town still shows plenty of scars.

Before we left Britain, we had been advised to take plenty of chocolate with us, partly because the East German chocolate was not very good, and partly because it was also expensive. I, therefore, had a good number of chocolate bars with me, and so did the other boys, which led to an interesting sidelight on the food situation in East Germany.

We were standing outside the station, opposite the Astoria, talking to a newspaper seller who had spent twenty-six years in America. When Bill Harris, the Middlesbrough half-back, pulled a bar of chocolate out of his pocket, the people standing round noticed at once, and, without embarrassment, asked him for some. We told them to wait, crossed the street to our hotel, and came back with the rest of our chocolate. Back at the station, we were surprised to find that a large crowd had gathered; the word had been spread that there was English chocolate about. Bill Harris, Dai Thomas of Swansea, Reg Davies of Newcastle and myself started to hand the bars out, but the crowd had become so large that the police were obliged to break it up.

There were further crowd scenes at the Astoria Hotel, on the morning of the match. Even though the stadium held 110,000, the match had been a "sell-out" days before. Indeed, we were told by East German officials that they would still have filled the stadium, even if it had held half-a-million. People kept coming to the hotel to see whether we had tickets to sell them, and they were prepared to pay any price we cared to name. Some of those touts you find outside Wembley Stadium on cup final day would have made a fortune here. Alas, we could help none of these supplicants; we had only two tickets each, which we had given to some members of a British variety show, on tour there.

Before our own match, we watched a junior game from the Press Box, midway up the terracing, then came the time to change. It took us nearly fifteen minutes to find the dressing-rooms, for despite the old legend of Teutonic thoroughness, nobody knew which room we were supposed to use. When we did at last find it, it was to discover an unexpected embarrassment. Two women were there, one of them the interpreter, another, a masseuse. It quickly became clear that if we were put out, they didn't mind in the least, and had no intention of going – so we just carried on with our changing.

Before the kick-off, there was another embarrassing moment – this time for John Charles. Brother Mel, standing at the end of our line, was holding a bouquet of flowers, which he was to give to John, who would present them to the captain of Germany. Dave Bowen, kidding Mel, and remembering what Arsenal's players had done when we were in Moscow and had received flowers, told him to throw the bouquet to somebody in the crowd. This, Mel did, and thus it came about that when the German captain shook hands beamingly with John and presented him with a bouquet, John found that his own hands were empty of anything to give him in return.

We should have won that match; indeed, the general opinion in Leipzig was that we would coast through it by five goals. I think they'd taken too much notice of the fact that we had had the better of Czechoslovakia. Anyway, we did score the first goal, through Mel Charles, who was leading our attack – and only six minutes had gone. Yet instead of gaining confidence with that encouraging start, it seemed to dribble away from us. The Germans gradually began to get a hold on the game, and they served up some very good football, even though only their centre forward, Willy Troger, really seemed dangerous. Throughout the match, I'm afraid he proved a bit of a handful for John Charles, and he was never afraid to try a shot.

Before half-time, an oddly streaky goal had put the Germans level. Just the same, I'm convinced they would never have scored it, had it not been for loose marking at a throw-in by our defence. Mayer, the outside-right, got the ball from the throw-in and crossed, hard and low. First Mel Hopkins, the long-legged Spurs left-back, missed the ball. That seemed to be that, but Wirth, running in from behind, cannoned into the ball which struck his boot and simply flew into the net. He looked amazed and I am quite sure he did not make contact by intention.

That was the score at half-time, when we went inside for the longest interval I can remember: it lasted twenty-five minutes. Both teams, the referee and the linesmen were transported up to the dressing-rooms by an enormous lift. It took us more than five minutes to get to ours, for the statutory fifteen minutes rest. Next, we had to wait for the lift to pick us up again. Then came another delay when Latyshev, the Russian referee, asked for the ball. It had been given to John Charles, John had left it in the dressing-room – and there was more delay while it was fetched.

That ball had already been a matter for contention, and may have had a little to do with our eventual defeat. It was brought in for our inspection before the match, Hungarian made, and much too soft. We asked for it to be more fully inflated. A few minutes later, it was brought back to us, but still we weren't satisfied and out it went again. Three times in all it was re-inflated, before we decided that it was now hard enough. Nevertheless, we did not play with that ball. Somewhere between the dressing-room and the field of play, it was apparently switched for a softer one; a mystery for Sherlock Holmes.

Was it the same for both sides? Certainly not. It is a known fact that continentals prefer to play with a soft ball, possibly because it suits their style. Here I might say that whenever Arsenal go on a European tour, we always take our own footballs with us and they're invariably blown up in the presence of our trainer, Billy Milne.

We played very badly in that second half, and another goal by Troger gave the match to East Germany. I don't think, on reflection, that we were unlucky in any way, though Tapscott, who collided with a photographer's box, and Bowen, who injured his back, were more or less passengers for the remainder of the game. I think it would, in fact, be fair to say that rarely has the Welsh team played so poorly. East Germany weren't good; that much we proved in the return game, when we beat them easily at Cardiff; a game which I unfortunately had to miss through injury.

I thought that our biggest failing was a tendency to keep the ball in the middle, instead of moving it out to the wings, where Cliff Jones had the beating of the German right-back, Buschner. Whenever John Charles had the ball he fraternally tried to pass it to Mel, and when they switched places, after Troger's goal, Mel reciprocated.

The result wasn't a very good augury for Prague. We knew it was going to be a much harder game on Czech soil, all the more so if they showed the finishing power which they'd belatedly revealed in the last ten minutes at Cardiff.

Down that dreary *autobahn* we drove again, this time to the East Berlin airport. I couldn't understand this, for if the coach had headed south instead of north, I am sure we'd have been in Prague within a fraction of the time it took us. The whole trip was a misery, anyway, for the smokers among us had run out of cigarettes. We had been told on our original B.E.A. plane that we were allowed to take only a certain fixed number of "smokes" behind the Iron Curtain, and this allocation was not sufficient to last our stay in Leipzig. It meant that during our last few hours there, we had to smoke the local brand – and nobody seemed to enjoy it. The worst thing of all was that we all thought that we should remain in the same wretched state for a week, until we touched down in Zurich.

Fortunately, rescue was at hand. The first people we saw when we arrived at Prague Airport were the West Ham United touring party, who had beaten us to it by just ten minutes. They were all standing outside the reception hall, awaiting customs clearance. As we walked up to them, Ernie Gregory, their hefty goalkeeper, did what might very easily have been a foolish thing; he pulled out a packet of English cigarettes. He nearly got killed in the rush. I know that the packet was quite empty when it was handed back to him.

Since the Hammers were staying at the same hotel as ourselves, they luckily were able to supply us with cigarettes until we met up with officials of the British Embassy, who carried on the charitable work.

I was greatly impressed by Prague, with its many wonderful buildings, their spires rising all over the city. It is called The City of a Hundred Spires, and though I did not stay long enough to count them, there must have been at least as many as that. Then there were the bridges, the most famous of which was the fourteenth-century Charles Bridge. They spanned the River Vlatava, on the bank of which stood a huge white statue of Stalin, over-looking the city. Mel Charles claimed that the Charles Bridge was named after him. Apparently nobody had told him its age....

Jimmy Murphy, and our trainer, Jack Jones of Wrexham, had us on the go all the time, determined that we should at least be as fit as the Czechs. Alas, the side could not be named because of the injuries which had afflicted us like a blight. Dave Bowen was definitely out, Derek Tapscott's injured ankle made him doubtful, and Reg Davies, his deputy, didn't feel too well, with a sore throat. One player alone was sure he would be playing – and he was not even with us! Ray

Daniel had just had his suspension lifted by the Football Association and was at once picked for the centre-half position, thus allowing John Charles to move up and strengthen the attack. He was to be flown out, and when Reg Davies cried off, too, a call went out for Des Palmer, the Swansea Town centre-forward. Poor Jimmy Murphy had to restrict his tactical planning to the left flank, while we waited for Palmer to arrive.

One consolation in all our difficulties was the kindness of that super athlete, Emil Zatopek, who took time off from his own athletic training to treat our blisters and other injuries; none so modest as the really great.

Alas, there was hardly any evening life in Prague to distract us. Once, we did try to see the English film *Romeo and Juliet*, which was showing there; but on inquiry, we found the cinema was booked up for six months in advance. So if Leipzig appeared to be starved of chocolate, then this other Iron Curtain country seemed to be starved of entertainment. Ironically, and as though to emphasize the contrast in deprivation, we visited a chocolate factory while we were in Prague. Apparently it's the most modern of its kind in the country and the Czechs were most anxious to show it off. All the workers there were women, and as we arrived in each department, there was always a girl waiting to greet us with a big bunch of flowers.

John Charles, as skipper, accepted these bouquets, and had the pleasant task of reciprocating with a kiss – which brought quite a bit of swooning at the benches. There were so many departments to go through that John eventually began to look like a perambulating harvest festival, and I took over from him at the next stop, handing the honour on to David Bowen, in turn. By the time we had been through the whole factory, I believe everybody in the party had been given a kiss. Lucky for us those Czech girls used no lipstick, so there weren't any tell-tale marks on our handkerchiefs to be explained to our wives when we reached home.

During the last three days in Prague, we did at last find something to entertain us in the evening, and it was the kind of entertainment most men like; boxing – the European Boxing Championships were being held. We spent every spare moment we had at them, for they went on all day, from half past eleven in the morning. Every Welshman in Prague was there on the second night, for Ron (Ponty) Davies, the solitary Welsh representative in the championships, was fighting. He got a great cheer from our small group when he entered the ring, and a still greater cheer when he was given the verdict. Alas, he lost his next contest – perhaps, who knows, because we were not there to cheer him on.

We were splendidly looked after by the British Embassy people, whom we met at one of West Ham United's matches. At a party one evening in the hotel of a diplomat working there, we were given some insight into what they have to put up with in an Iron Curtain country. A tiny hole was pointed out to us, near the floor. This, we were told, led to a concealed microphone. There was no way of getting at it; and apparently every similar room, occupied by a diplomat, had one. Some of them used to get round it by playing their gramophones loud up against it whenever they had anything private to discuss.

In Prague, as in Leipzig, our match had attracted huge interest; the Czechs had not previously played in the World Cup since the war. Demand was increased by the fact that the stadium where the match was to be played held a paltry 45,000. Less than a hundred yards away stood another stadium, irony of ironies, with a capacity of 250,000. Alas, though it had a so-called soccer pitch inside it, this consisted of red ash, badly cut up by having been used for stock-car racing and stunt driving.

An additional use, we were told, was for parachute jumping displays. Soccer had a look-in only when the stadium was used for training purposes, when the other grounds in Prague were engaged, round and about the locality. To us players it seemed such a waste of a good stadium. With turf laid and a few repairs it could quickly be made into a ground superior to anything we have in this country.

No wonder, in these circumstances, that three Czech fans decided to make their own way into the football ground, the night before the match. Police caught them digging a tunnel under the outside wall, and they were arrested. Other Czechs contented themselves with besieging us for tickets, which we just hadn't got to spare, though we contented some of them by throwing them packets of chewing gum. This was in terrific demand, especially among the children, who were perpetually asking for "chewy".

As for the next match, a rather high wind threatened its quality. It did not seem to worry the Czechs. They were playing good football and shooting, too, though without bothering me greatly. We had a wonderful chance of scoring the first goal; if we had done so, there might have been a vast difference in the game. John Charles pulled down a clearance from right-back, Dai Thomas, and raced through for thirty yards. He was just outside the penalty area, with a clear path to goal, when Novak, the Czech left-half, came across and tripped him up. Even then, I think he would have recovered and gone on to score, but all that must be speculation, for the referee did not play the "advantage rule". Instead, we were awarded a free kick, and though John blasted it at goal, it merely came back from the wall of Czech defenders.

That was a piece of bad luck. The Czechs' first goal represented an even worse one. It came after twenty-two minutes. Mel Hopkins, who had been playing outside-right

Gadjos extremely well, was beaten by him for the first time, out by the touch-line. Gadjos worked his way up the by-line, then drove the ball strongly across goal. It hit Ray Daniel on the head and rocketed into the net like an atomic warhead; there wasn't much hope of stopping that one. Poor Ray buried his head in his hands, and I tried to console him by saying, "Never mind, Ray, you couldn't have got out of the way of it." What worried us most was the thought that this goal might shake his confidence, because until then, despite his lack of match practice, he had not put a foot wrong.

But Ray has the right temperament, and quickly proved that he is not the sort of person to be worried by an "own goal". Soon, he was once more playing with all the confidence in the world.

We tried desperately hard to equalize, and twice centres from Cliff Jones nearly brought a goal. Bill Harris was playing a lovely game at left-half, supplying Jones and Vernon with pass after perfect pass, while John Charles gave up his deep-lying position to move to the assault. Alas, as soon as the ball was moved into the middle, the Czech defenders were on hand to deal with it.

In the second half, we had the wind behind us, but instead of giving us the initiative, we found that playing into the wind appeared to suit the Czechs. Their half-backs got a stranglehold on the game, and a beautiful move brought them their second goal after twenty minutes. An overhead kick by Kraus, their outside-left, went to Moravicka. Kraus darted quickly into the six-yard box for the return, which came without a second wasted. The winger hit the ball, first time, on to the far post and into the net; a move carried out so fast that I don't think we really knew what hit us. Wales 0, Czechoslovakia 2. We'd lost both our matches, and our qualifying chances were slim indeed.

I think we fell, where we had previously stood, by John Charles, for I can safely say that these were the worst two games I have ever seen the big fellow play for Wales. He seemed to be stale, a condition which could possibly be put down to the number of trips he had made before the game; twice to Italy and once to Holland, on tour with Leeds. Yet, later in the summer, he showed superb form on the Juventus tour of Sweden. Another possible explanation is that he was worried and upset by all the publicity contingent on his big money transfer deal, which was to make him the richest British player in football history.

Our agony as prolonged a little when, as I've mentioned, a Charles-less team beat the East Germans at Cardiff, but the Czechs drubbed the Germans twice, and that was that. By way of some consolation, at least we had the hospitality of the Embassy people, after our defeat in Prague. Ray Daniel was not deterred by the microphones. He went up to one of the holes, pulled out the wooden block which concealed it, and shouted, "You, down there, hand on a few seconds, and I'll sing you the Red Flag." There was no reply to his offer.

But an English girl at the Embassy had apparently got a better response. Coming into her new hotel room, she commented, "Oh, those curtains; they're filthy!" When she came back that evening the curtains had been changed.

Apropos of matches between Wales and the Continent, I always remember how one of them was the occasion of the strongest, yet probably most effective, massage I have ever been given. We were playing Yugoslavia at Cardiff. On the Friday, during our last training session, I went over a low wall to collect a ball which I had tipped over the bar and, coming back, succeeded in bashing my knee against it. It swelled up most painfully, and there were real doubts of whether I should be able to play. To the rescue came Bill Dodman, who was with our party, and had once upon a time trained the famous scrapper, Johnny Basham. "Come up in your room," he said, but when he got me there, it was to find that he was without the bottle of specially made-up liniment which he always carried.

"What can I use?" he said – and all he could think of was Brylcreem. I had a bottle of it with me, and he massaged my knee with this strange substitute-embrocation! Next morning the swelling had gone and the knee was as right as could be.

The departure of John Charles certainly left a great gap in our Welsh side, though perhaps we had been inclined to play too much to him. The team clicked against the East Germans, in its first match of the 1957-8 season, and I watched from the stand on of the best exhibitions I have ever seen from Wales. If only we could have pulled it out in Leipzig.

We weren't so good against England, a few weeks later, on the same ground, and I'm afraid I was in goal that day. England, in fact, scored four without reply, though in my view it was another example of how an incident, just one solitary event, can change the whole face of a soccer game. It was another own goal that did it. We had opened the game quite well and, for the first seven minutes, we had more of the play. Then Mel Hopkins chased after a ball, hotly attended by big Derek Kevan, the England inside-right. I called to Mel to leave the ball as I came out to collect it. Instead, he got his foot to it and sent it past me for England's opening goal. I may add that the through pass had originally been made by Johnny Haynes, who scored two of England's goals himself.

The first came from a fairly hard drive, just inside the post. I dived for the ball but it seemed to be possessed, for as it approached the goal, when I was already in mid-air, it started swinging. It was much too late for me to do anything about changing direction by that time. So far, indeed, did the ball swing that when it eventually hit the net, it was the inside portion. I'm afraid we just did not click as a team and, as the match went on, so it became more and more obvious what was in store for us. I had no disagreement with our chairman, Milwyn Jenkins, when he said after the game that it was the worst performance he'd ever seen by a Welsh side.

In Prague, when the score was 2-0 against us, I heard that Jimmy Murphy whipped up the ball when it went out of play, put it under his coat, and announced, "That's it. They won't score again." But I'm afraid it wouldn't have done us much good against that powerful-looking England team. In the second half, Johnny Haynes got another, this time with a long shot which zipped in off the greasy surface. Perhaps I would have got at it on a normal day, but the churned up goal mouth prevented me from achieving the necessary take-off, and the six inches or so that I lost were vital – and fatal.

Tom Finney's, however, was the best goal of all. He came in from the left wing and beat three men before cracking the ball in.

After all that, it was a bit of a relief to go up to Hampden the next month with a question-mark side and, in true Red Dragon tradition, hold the Scots to a draw. We were really worth a win. Terry Medwin, shifted from the right-wing back to his old Swansea position of centre-forward, moved all over the field and led the Scottish defence a terrible dance, with plenty of backing from Cliffy Jones. If soccer can be an odd game, then international soccer is even odder.

12
A SCOTTISH POUND NOTE

When Arthur Shaw left Arsenal for Watford, Highbury lost its leading practical joker. Certainly, things haven't been quite the same.... Of the many jokes and ruses which Arthur succeeded in perpetrating, perhaps the one best remembered at Highbury was brought off at the expense of Commander Bone, one of our directors.

It was May 1953, and we were in Glasgow for the Coronation Cup. Driving away from the golf course at Skelmorlie, in the team coach, Arthur Shaw approached the commander with a Scottish one-pound note in his hand; and Commander Bone, of course, is a banker. "Look at this, Commander," he said. "Stage money. I found it on the golf course."

"No, no," said the commander, speaking seriously, as bankers will of money, "it's a Scottish pound note."

"It's stage money!" Arthur insisted. "There's a whole bundle of it up there; we were kicking it about all over the place."

"I'll give you ten shillings for it," Commander Bone offered.

"No," said Arthur, "I wouldn't take it off you." And saying this, he put the one-pound into his other hand, and threw out of the window – a crumpled envelope.

"Idiot!" cried the commander. "You've thrown a pound note away."

"It's only stage money," said Arthur.

Later that day, Joe Mercer was driving several of the boys along that road in his car. "Wouldn't it be funny," somebody said, not too hopefully, "if we saw Commander

Bone, looking for the one-pound note." And sure enough – there he was, eyes on the ground, looking meticulously in the road for the quid that never was. Joe Mercer collapsed helplessly over the steering-wheel, leaning on the horn, which gave out a tremendous Bronx cheer. The commander looked up at them.

"I've never seen so many cigarette and toffee papers in my life," he said.

Once again, new faces were appearing at Highbury. After the 1953 league victory, there was something of a transition period, as old names disappeared, and more and more young footballers were drafted into the team; Danny Clapton, Jimmy Bloomfield, David Herd, Vic Groves, Stan Charlton, Joe Haverty – most of them forwards, as you can see.

Jimmy Bloomfield is a Londoner, who came to us from Brentford, and played on the left-wing for a while, before moving to his proper position at inside-forward. Slimly built, he still has a great capacity for work, moves the ball beautifully at times, and has greatly improved his passing. Off field, he has the Cockney's confidence – like Vic Groves and Danny Clapton; shrewd but not immodest, a player who takes his football seriously.

So does David Herd, a talented son of a famous father – Alex, the old Herts and Manchester City inside-right, renowned for a cannon-ball shot in his right boot. David hits the ball hard as well, from inside-right or centre-forward, and he can be devastating in the air. He's a studious type of player, no doubt through being brought up by Father in the ways of the game. On occasion, they actually turned out together in the Stockport County League team.

David would be the first to admit that his left foot is not as strong as his right; I certainly would not describe him as a two-footed player. He takes quite a lot of ribbing from the boys over his "swinger".

This young forward, who treats five-a-side games as seriously as he would a cup final, who also plays tennis, cricket and golf, is our Players' Union delegate. Yet he's a shy, quiet lad, and although, as delegate, he speaks up for us, it is very rarely that he speaks up for himself.

That makes him a contrast with Vic Groves. When Vic arrived from Leyton Orient in 1955, together with Stan Charlton, the old bugbear of introducing afflicted the shyer Charlton, but not this bubbling Londoner. Stan used to sit all my himself in the plunge-bath, while Vic chattered away to everybody; before we found out that, in the old English tradition, he was still waiting to be introduced.

Vic's a very deceptive player. At times, probably owing to his rather large frame, he can appear to be awkward and slow. But he's always dangerous with foot or head, when in range of goal, and he seemed to have a specially good understanding with Derek Tapscott. He loves talking soccer, trying new moves, and he has a very good knowledge of the game. In the dressing-room, he keeps us amused with his singing; away from Highbury, he loves fishing, though this pastime may suffer eventually, as a result of his growing interest in golf. Perhaps fishing, with its air of timelessness, is best adapted for Vic, though. I'm sure he'd be late for his own funeral.

Stan Charlton is less ebullient; and he's a useful back to have in any side. He never admits to being beaten, and a winger who gets past Stan can expect to be tackled by him again before he has made much ground, such is his power of recovery. His heading is not all that it should be; nevertheless, if I were picking the team, I should always like to see him in front of me, in the comforting certainty that he won't give up. As a goalkeeper, I admit that he gives me extra confidence.

Off the field, though you'd never think it, this likeable chap is preparing for his after-football days by studying ladies' hairdressing, in company with Orient's goalie, David Groombridge. Stan is always ready to make friends, and he and I are usually to be found together, when we travel away.

He is, of course, a very powerful man physically, built strong and square, like a bull or a Sherman tank. Little Joe Haverty, on the other hand, looks like the perennial schoolboy and, despite his Irish international status, mixes chiefly with the younger players at Highbury.

The Highbury crowd love this little outside-left, probably because sports fans always have an affection for a good little 'un. He's a clever ball player, who overdoes it a little, I think, thus tending to hold up the forward-line, while another bad habit is that of playing the ball backwards. Joe has his own way of avoiding a tackle – by jumping. Perhaps that is why he once received a Christmas card with a kangaroo on it...

If ever you want to try out a new joke, Joe's your man; no matter how bad it may be, you can be certain that he will laugh. Yet when he tries to tell a joke himself, he can never get to the end of it for his own laughter. As so often happens, he is regarded by the rest of us as the young boy of the team, owing to his lack of inches and his youthful appearance.

Danny Clapton, on the right, is a more orthodox player; over a short distance, the fastest runner we have at Highbury, though he could show this a bit more on the field. Danny himself wrote to the club, asking for a trial. He came through it, and graduated to the league team through the "A" and Combination sides, like myself; a real High "product".

In my opinion he could play himself into the England team whenever he put his mind to it, such is his potential ability. He has quite good ball control, and shoots fairly hard, too; he likes to call his shots "thunderbolts", and if he cut in to shoot more often, I think he could be the complete winger. Once he liked to have the ball passed straight to his feet, but I think he now realizes that the ball pushed inside the full-back enables him to run onto it, without having first to beat his man.

Off the field, Danny doesn't say a great deal, but he thinks very deeply and he's a quick-witted type. He has pet names for most of us at Highbury; mine, since my hair is receding slightly, is "Yul Brynner".

In recent years, we've been involved in some epic cup-ties. Wembley, at times, has seemed just beyond the horizon – but the sixth round has proved a very high hurdle. On the other hand, there was that third round affair against Bedford Town, in 1956, when it seemed that Arsenal's debacle against Walsall, in 1933, would be surpassed; that we would be knocked out, ignominy of ignominies, by a non-league team. We weren't – but it was a very, very near thing.

I've said before that we don't like playing against lowly-placed teams. At Highbury, where Bedford held us to a 2-2 draw, I wasn't playing – Con Sullivan was in goal, and I watched from the stand. I must say I thought we'd go up to Bedford and walk the replay – it was only a wonderful display by Pope, in goal, that allowed them to hold us. But my optimism wasn't justified – to say the least. On their own ground – and I was playing, this time – they turned out to be a different team, a team that tackled hard and chased everything; a team that used just the sort of tactics to put off a First Division side. They seemed to be playing fifteen men, and the crowd on that tiny ground, roaringly enthusiastic, was almost as good as a sixteenth.

They scored first, too. Yates got it, shooting into the corner of the net from about fourteen yards out. The ground was rather rough as it was, and spread sawdust, mingled with tiny blocks of wood, did not make it smoother. The ball bobbled along the ground, just out of my reach – and all Bedford seemed to explode with joy.

Not long afterwards, they got the ball in the net again – but this time, thank goodness, it was an offside affair. The Polish winger, Felix Staroscik, came in along the by-line. He slipped the ball past me as I dived at his feet, and a Bedford forward standing right under the bar, tapped the ball home. The referee gave him offside – and the crowd, naturally, were not inclined to agree.

Bedford were chasing and running, chasing and running, having more of the play while, as the same time, Pope was playing another blinder in goal. There were five minutes left, and I thought it was all up with us. I heard afterwards that even the Governor had lost all hope – and he doesn't give up very easily. Then Grovesey leaped into the air to head a superb goal from Jimmy Bloomfield's cross – and we were breathing again.

In extra time, Bedford once more got the ball into the net, and once more it was given offside. The crowd didn't like that, either, and they began throwing great chunks of clinker on to the pitch. The target was the referee, but the barrage mostly landed around my feet; much too near for comfort. I picked up a clinker four inches across and showed it to the referee; I don't like to think what would have happened if it had hit me on the head. But he had a word with the police, the barrage was discontinued, and Derek Tapscott scored another goal to win us one of the stiffest fights we've ever had. It was a real scare, and Bedford had fought magnificently.

We went out, after an easy home win against the Villa and a very good away win against Charlton (2-0) in front of a huge, swaying crowd, to Birmingham City, the eventual finalists. Stan Charlton got our only goal, with a rocketing long shot, after a corner. Though the game was played at Highbury, I'm afraid City had much the better of it, that day.

Nineteen fifty-seven, and it was almost the mixture as before; the sixth round, and defeat at Highbury by another Birmingham team – this time in the shape of West Bromwich Albion. But the complexion of the match was a great deal different, for this was one we should never, never have lost.

In the first game, up at The Hawthorns, you'll remember that I had refused a ticket to my mother-in-law. But I knew she would probably be in the crowd, and I swear this was responsible, silly as it may seem, for my jittery play in the early stages. We were not very lucky that day, for Ronnie Allen forced Albion's first goal in over my arm, the ball just rolling over the top of it, as I attempted to block it, while the second goal spun in off the chest of unlucky Len Wills.

These goals, however, seemed quite unexceptionable by comparison with that which put Albion ahead in the replay, two minutes after half-time. Our forwards should have had the game well won by then. With Danny Clapton beating Len Millard for speed, time and again, the chances were there, but we somehow were not exploiting them. Once, a centre by Danny was dropped by Jim Sanders, Albion's goalie – but he recovered in time to smother the ball, as Derek Tapscott raced in for the kill. A couple of minutes from the interval, Derek was through on his own, when it seemed easier to score than miss – but he missed.

Then came Albion's goal. Allen, Albion's deep-lying centre-forward, received the ball just outside our penalty-area, and pushed it through to Whitehouse, who was standing about seven yards from goal, and at least five yards offside. He stopped the ball, moved it forward about a yard, steadied himself, then crashed it hard and low into the net, on my left-hand side. We weren't unduly worried, because, in common with 60,000 spectators, we saw that the linesman's flag was waving. As I picked the ball out of the net, I glanced over towards the linesman, and saw with relief that his flag was still up.

You can imagine, then, that we Arsenal players felt when we saw Mr. J. G. Williams, of Nottingham, the referee, pointing towards the centre, for a goal. Despite our strong protests, he refused to go over to consult the linesman. The goal stood, Danny Clapton missed a penalty – no thunderbolt, this, but a half-hearted, side-foot shot along the ground – Derek Kevan scored another, and a consolation goal from Cliff Holton was all we had to show. We were out.

Though most people blamed the referee for allowing that disputed goal, I myself still blame the linesman. Afterwards, Mr. Williams stated in an interview that he did not see the linesman flag. Perhaps he never saw the flag up, in which case he was perfectly right to allow the goal. Yet I think that the linesman, once having flagged, should have had the courage of his convictions – and kept it up. Even Whitehouse, the scorer, admitted that he was offside and added, "I do not know if anybody played me onside by touching the ball." Nobody that I saw, anyway.

But...the goal stood, the score stood, and, once again, there was no Wembley for us. I still feel that if the goal had been disallowed, we would have gone on to win the cup. But maybe that is only prejudice.

A dramatic moment during the Wales v Scotland match at Cardiff in October 1956. Alf Sherwood (3) and Roy Paul are my fellow defenders.

One of my hobbies is making musical boxes. Here I am putting the finishing touches to one in my home.

Four Arsenal players who played for Wales in the same eleven. Left to right: Dave Bowen, myself, Derek Tapscott and Walley Barnes.

A tense moment as Vic Keeble (later with West Ham) prepares to let fly for Newcastle United in a match at Highbury. Cliff Holton is about to challenge for possession.

John Charles greets the Welsh players at Tel Aviv on arrival for the World Cup game, January 1958.

I take a picture of John Charles at Leipzig, 1957.

"This one is mine!" I can almost hear myself saying it as I take the ball off the foot of Taylor (Preston). Baxter (Preston) is just behind me. February 1957.

All pals together! Two Arsenal colleagues – Bowden and Dodgin – leap with me as I punch clear during a match against Manchester United at Highbury, 1956.

13
WHY NOT BRITAIN?

When people ask me what I am going to do when my playing days are over, my answer surprises them. "I don't know," I say, "but I shan't be staying in football. Fifteen years in the game is quite enough; I want to do something else."

I couldn't tell you what it is, though probably it will be some sort of business. I've already tried my hand at running a weight-training gymnasium with Bill Watson, who has trained a number of soccer clubs, Arsenal, Doncaster and West Bromwich among them. But I believe in a periodic change of scenery. Playing soccer is fine, but I would never want to coach, train or manage a team.

As a player, there are a number of things which I would like to see changed; transfers and contracts being top of the list. In this, I imagine I have the support of every professional in the league. So far as I am concerned, soccer players *are* slaves, for my definition of slavery is the absence of freedom. Professional footballers are *not* free to leave their clubs after any given period, for, as everybody knows, they have only to be offered the minimum wage to be retained.

In my view, the maximum wage should be scrapped, and every player should be made free to negotiate his own contract with his club. I completely reject the argument that there would be discontent among lower-paid players, who might say, "Why should Kelsey get more than me, when he is playing badly?" I reject it, because there seems to me absolutely no reason why that player should know what I am earning. If I am taking in £30 a week, that's surely my business; my contract would and should have been negotiated secretly. When I was working as a painter and rigger, I had no idea what the other members of the crew were earning – and vice versa. Yet if you asked the man next door to me, he could probably tell you to within a few hundred pounds just what I had in the bank, for everybody knows what footballers earn, directly from the game – and why on earth should they?

As for the contracts, they should be made for a specific period with, if you like, an option for renewal, so that the club could either discard the player if he was not doing well, or the player could command more money, if his value to them had increased. Every footballer should be paid what he is worth by whatever club is prepared to pay it to him.

Another thing I'd like to see is more coaching in soccer. Every club should have a coach, just as they do abroad. And coaching should be started as soon as a boy leaves school – or sooner. In fact I believe that we should set up sports schools all over the country, the "fees" for their pupils being paid by the league clubs. Let us say that I'm a promising player, in my early teens, and a certain club wants me to sign, on leaving ordinary school. They might send me, until I have reached the minimum signing age of seventeen, to one of these soccer schools. When I "come of age", I could sign as a full-time pro, or, alternatively, stay a little while longer at the soccer school. After all, the club would be paying me, anyway, if I were on their ground staff, and although this might work out to be a bit dearer, it would surely be worth it in the long run.

After seeing the sports schools in Germany, I am convinced that the Football Association should have its own establishments; not be obliged to use the Lilleshall centre, for example, which belongs to the Central Council of Physical Recreation. And it seems to me silly that the F.A. and Football League should continue to turn down money from the pools, when they not only need such centres as these, but should also have their own stadium.

Any other complains? Not many; but I would like to see firmer action taken against the Killer Players. There aren't many of them about, thank goodness; those there are, are well known, and could easily be stamped on. I remember an Arsenal game, away from home, which took place not long ago, in which a youngster was making his debut for us. Within fifteen minutes he had been kicked off the field; and I'm convinced that the foul was quite deliberate. We must get rid of that type of player as though he were a soccer scorpion.

Then, I agree with those who believe the time has come to field a Great Britain team in international tournaments. After all, we are only a small country, whatever the size of our population; we can hardly expect to hold our own with nations whose populations so outnumber ours, when we split our available resources into four. If we fielded a Great Britain side, and all the home associations pulled their weight (as they sadly failed to do for the Belfast match against Europe, in 1955), then I believe we would really go places. And such a team ought to be taken away for a full month's training; not for one, inadequate day.

In goal, give me of two blond giants; Harry Gregg, of Manchester United and Ireland, the man who wears a torn old cap which has been with him since his days as a joiner, or Scotland's Tommy Younger. Younger I have already discussed; Gregg is well up in the same class, and his display against England at Wembley in 1957 – though I saw it only on television – will be remembered for many a year.

At right-back, I think Alex Parker of Falkirk and Scotland is the finest in the British Isles. He's steady, times a tackle well, and likes to use the ball; no aimless kicking for this able player. If he can move the ball "short" to a wing-half, he'd rather do that than give it a boot up the field. He can shoot, too, on occasion, as I've cause to know!

Left-back is not, today, the easiest position to fill, but Mel Hopkins always gives me a great feeling of confidence when playing behind him, and he gets my vote.

For right-half, it must be Danny Blanchflower, master schemer and theorist. Though he walks into the team, I would like to give a solid pat on the back to Ronnie Clayton, of Blackburn and England. He's less spectacular but more intelligent than the late Duncan Edwards, quite firm in the tackle, and determined always to use the ball, which is what you want from your wing-halves.

Billy Wright has shown himself the perfect centre-half, a player who could provide an example for any youngster wanting to play pro football; a wonderful player, and, despite his innumerable caps, always easy to get on with, off the field.

At left-half, my choice falls on Bill Slater, of Wolves and England, who was one of the few English successes in the World Cup.

In attack, Tom Finney would be my outside-right; the man who has everything Stanley Matthews has had, plus a shot. I would prefer him to Stan on the grounds of his finishing, even though his ball control isn't quite in the same class, and his best position, for me, at least, is centre-forward. Tom's speed off the mark is very little behind the Maestro's, and...what we want from forwards is goals!

Inside-right, tricky little Bobby Collins of Celtic and Scotland, the forward who started as a pocket-sized right-winger, and has cleverly adapted his play. Bobby has the control one expects from a very good little 'un, and plenty of football brains, as well.

For centre-forward I have no hesitation in saying John Charles, though he may be a Juventus player. Personally I still think his best position is centre-half, but Big John can play brilliantly in any position – including goal! In any event, I always feel as safe as houses behind this massive man.

Johnny Haynes must be the inside-left. His main asset, of course, is pushing that through ball, and no player in the country can make that pass so well. He is that ideal inside-forward, the one whose pass beats a player for you, and does half your work, while he is a fair shot, as well. Off the field, I've always found Johnny very pleasant, and if the papers have occasionally hinted of his being "big-headed", then it's a characteristic I've never noticed. To talk to him, you wouldn't think he could cross anybody.

Finally, on the left-wing, I would like Cliff Jones, the Welsh Express, who can outstrip almost any back in the world. What a partnership he could form with Johnny Haynes to give him the passes to run on to!

As for myself, I hope I have a few years in the game yet. There are two ambitions which I would like to fulfil at Wembley; to play there in a Welsh team which beats England, and to play there in an Arsenal team which wins the cup.

No doubt we shall see....

14
ARSENAL UNDER FIRE

Northampton Town 3, Arsenal 1. Most of you who read this will be pretty familiar with the result by now. You will not need me to remind you that it was a third-round cup tie in the 1958 edition of the F.A. cup tournament.

Oceans of print and wordage were poured out by the Press on the subject of our defeat by a quick, energetic Northampton side in which one star forward, Tebutt, was actually making his debut (he scored a goal, too!). During the week which followed that disastrous match, I am quite sure people must have been tired of hearing about the Arsenal, and what was allegedly wrong with them. Certainly we at Highbury could scarcely be expected to know; if we had done so, we would presumably have set matters right.

Of one thing I am quite certain: the Press should have left us alone. I am too young to remember anything about that Walsall defeat in 1933, but in my own experience, no cup result has ever caused such a crescendo of controversy. Sunderland is a club with a great tradition, too, a tradition which goes back much farther than Arsenal's, yet I don't recall a great deal of fuss being made after their cup defeat at Yeovil in 1949.

One of the points raised by the majority of critics seemed to be that the team lacked major personalities, and that we should go out to buy certain players whose names they were good enough to suggest to us. Many names were mentioned. All were the names of leading footballers of international standard. These critics seemed to be suffering from the delusion that Arsenal's directors had the power to go to any club in Britain, tell them, "Look here, we want so-and-so. How much?" and conclude the deal as if by magic, as though to say, "Wrap him up: we'll take him home with us." Whether the player concerned was ready to move, and whether his club was prepared to release him if he did agree, wasn't taken into apparent consideration. It seems to me that whenever a leading player asks for a transfer, Arsenal are invariably "interested", without anyone at Highbury knowing a thing about the matter!

There is one very good reason why I believe few if any star players will come to Highbury, and that is that the Arsenal do everything legally. There have been a number of cases in which Arsenal have been interested in star players, and that interest has been reciprocated on the player's side. But when it comes down to brass tacks, and it has been made clear that there's nothing in it for the players themselves, then interest has suddenly melted away. Arsenal just will not pay under the counter. If they did, believe me, they would be the greatest side in the world, for every top player would want to join them.

But let us return to the game at Northampton. In all fairness, I think that the Cobblers thoroughly deserved to win. They did not play the kick and rush game which we expected them to; indeed, it was all the more humiliating that, on the day, they should play much better football than we ourselves. There was an exception: in the last twenty minutes of the first half we were right on top and, with the score 1-1, should have taken the lead. David Herd was through with a clear shot at goal, and although he let fly, he was unlucky enough to see his drive hit the base of the post. I am sure that, had his shot gone in, it would have been a different tale: but then, who can tell? Much though I disliked being in the side beaten by Northampton, I felt sorry for them during the following week. No praise for them in the papers. Nothing about how well they played to beat

Arsenal: only how badly Arsenal had played to lose to lowly Northampton.

Even our own programme had something to say about the match, on the occasion of our next home game, and it was not very complimentary, I'm afraid, as far as the players were concerned. We were virtually accused of lack of effort, in the words, "the vital difference between the two teams was effort". It couldn't have been much more clearly stated. Coming as it did from within the club, I thought it very unfair, and so did most of the team which played – and lost – at Northampton. I am sure that everyone who played for us in that match gave all he had to give. Whether or not the ball ran for us is wholly another matter. The ball is round, after all – and it can run anywhere.

The same programme article referred back to the Walsall defeat, twenty-five years before, remarking, that Northampton was a different "kettle of fish". But *why*? Did the beaten team of 1933 put in a greater effort than ourselves? True, it fielded four reserves, but were not players of the calibre of David Jack, Cliff Bastin and Alex James still playing?

Another portion of the same article really made me feel ashamed. We had been having rather a lean time, prior to our cup defeat, and the writer of the article gave what he thought to be the reason. I quote:

> *"The present position is the culmination of an insidious trend dating back to 1952. The team then being carried forward to reasonable success by determination and the superb captaincy of Joe Mercer."*

Nineteen fifty-two-three was the season when Arsenal last won the league. This, I suppose, is what they regard as merely "reasonable success". Probably if we had won the cup as well, that season, they might have said: "Not bad, but room for improvement!"

The part that hurt me most, however, was that it appeared that the blame was being shifted on to the late Tom Whittaker, in so far as he was manager of the team, when the slide began. Poor Tom was incapable of defending himself from the slight.

Finally, at a time when the Press were beginning to leave us alone, all this gave them cause to write about us again. The programme went on to say that we would "come back" as soon as the publicity had died down; yet here they were feeding the very flames! For the next few days, we were continually reminded by the Press of the article which appeared in the programme – in our own programme. On the day of its publication, we were beaten 3-2 at home by Blackpool after being two goals in the lead. I wouldn't like to say whether the article had an upsetting effect on the team, but I do know that I myself was feeling none too happy about what I had just read.

On the credit side, however, the club certainly made an excellent appointment, if it was effort they wanted, when they made Ron Greenwood chief coach. Ron, a redoubtable and hard tackling centre-half with Chelsea, Bradford, Brentford and Fulham, then manager of Eastbourne United, was introduced to us in the dressing-room on the first day of his appointment, with all the boys and the whole staff present.

His job was to introduce new training methods at Highbury, and very well he had been doing it, too. Training today is not the dreary lapping that it used to be. Now it is interesting, something that we enjoy. Full of ideas, Ron always has something new for us; no two days of training ever seem to be the same, under him.

One thing for which we shall always be grateful to him is that we now get on to the pitch to play our practice games. In the past, before Ron's arrival, we had to play them on the training ground, which was too small, besides being dangerous to bare knees, with its hard red surface. Now, if the pitch is dry, then on the pitch we play. In time I am quite sure that Ron Greenwood will restore the "glamour" tag to Arsenal, and he will not need luck: he is one of the best coaches I have ever met.

He has a fine way of putting things over, and to me, one of his greatest assets is the ability to keep one interested. Nor will he ever ask you to do anything he cannot do himself. Though our training today is harder than it ever was, we hardly notice the difference now – thanks to the Greenwood system.

15
REPRIEVE FOR WALES

For "Lucky Arsenal", I suppose there are some who would now substitute "Lucky Wales". Certainly we seemed to be well and truly out of the World Cup when Czechoslovakia hammered the East Germans. Instead, F.I.F.A. suddenly decided that Israel, whose opponents – Egypt, Turkey, and Indonesia – had all refused to play them – must fight her way to Sweden. That meant a draw among every country which had finished second in its qualifying group; with the proud exception of Uruguay who, as former winners on two occasions, probably felt it beneath their dignity to come in "by the back door" in this slightly dubious way.

The draw was made at F.I.F.A. H.Q. in Zurich and, with the odds at about seven to one against Wales, I did not even bother to listen to the radio that evening. Thus it was that the news – once more in my career! – leaped out of the morning papers to hit me, when my wife brought them up in the usual way, while I was still lying in bed. Wales were to play Israel: the headlines blared: WALES' SECOND CHANCE IN WORLD CUP.

I thought at once that we must now be certainties to pass on to Sweden. I knew that we must meet the Israelis twice, and I didn't expect them to be too difficult to beat. After all, so far as football is concerned, they must be ranked one of the youngest countries in the world: they have had an international team for only ten years, and they are still amateurs.

By agreement between the two countries, it was arranged to play the first match at the Ramat Gan Stadium, Tel Aviv, on 15 January, 1958, and the return at Cardiff, on 5 February. As soon as the draw was known, Welsh F.A.

officials got in touch with Juventus to arrange the release of John Charles to play in both matches. This was duly and generously granted and, with the return of Ivor Allchurch to the side, after missing the last half-dozen matches through injury, it was a full-strength Wales eleven that would make the trip to Tel Aviv.

The welcome we received when we got to the airport, besieged by press men and photographers, meant that we didn't reach our hotel until 1a.m., but the warmth of the reception made it worth the loss of a few hours sleep.

Training the next day wasn't too popular. We had flown out of the fog and cold of London to a temperature of eighty degrees. Graham Vearncombe, our reserve keeper, found it altogether too much. He collapsed, and had to be revived in the cool of the dressing-room.

The stadium did not impress us much. We were told that building had begun eight years before, and from what we could see, it still had not been completed. There were grassy mounds behind each goal, seating down one side of the ground – and nothing at all at the other, which was quite open. A barbed wire barrier was there to keep spectators in their places. The atmosphere of a besieged camp was added to by the five-feet deep moat which surrounded the pitch. This, itself, had a surprising amount of short grass growing on it, but the four corners were in poor condition: it appeared as though a vehicle with caterpillar tracks had been making short cuts across them, churning up what there was of the turf.

To my great regret, we were robbed of a trip to Jerusalem and the holy places because someone had forgotten to bring footballs for the morning session; ball training consequently had to take place in the afternoon, instead.

John Charles and I shared a room; by now, the big fellow was established and recognized as the finest centre-forward in Italy. Yet even on a football field, I don't think I have ever seen John move so fast as he did on our hotel balcony.... Lizards were primarily to blame. We had just finished breakfast, out in the sun, and I put my head round the corner of the balcony to see if there were any lizards there. The whole place swarmed with them: lizard hunting, indeed, had almost become a team recreation. Sure enough, there were about a dozen of the creatures, all between ten and fifteen inches long, about a foot from my face.

"Put your head round the corner," I told John, "and have a look at those lizards." He obeyed, and was putting his head round very slowly, in order not to frighten the lizards, when a bird darted suddenly from the side of the building, missing his face by inches. I've never seen so large a man move so quickly; he was so sure that a lizard had jumped out at him. It was a long time before John would look round that corner, again.

What enthusiasm there was for this match! We stripped in our hotel, reckoning the dressing-room accommodation to be too restricted. Traffic congestion was such that although we left with twenty minutes to spare, we were still fifteen minutes late for the kick-off.

The week before the match, in a broadcast to Israel, I forecast the score at 4-1 in our favour. Had it not been for the home goalkeeper Chodoroff, I should probably been right. Ivor Allchurch played the best game I have ever seen him play for Wales, and, after the first ten minutes, it was mostly one way: but Chodoroff showed us why he has held his place ever since Israel began playing international football. Ivor scored one of our two goals with a beauty from twenty-five yards, after half-time; a thirty-yard drive from Dave Bowen, captain on the day, surprised Chodoroff for the second.

The Israeli keeper stood between us and a cricket score in the return at Cardiff, too. Here, the conditions were right against the Israeli team. Heavy rain the previous night threatened a muddy ground, but a wind blowing all morning dried out the pitch considerably. Before the match, Gigi Peronace, John Charles's constant shadow, came to our dressing-room to wish us luck.

"The Israeli's won't like this wet ground," he said, walking across to me.

"I won't be comfortable out there, myself," I told him, explaining how difficult an orange ball can be to handle, when it is wet.

"It won't worry you," Peronace replied – he once kept goal for an Italian Third League team. "I think you are an old fox, in goal."

Chodoroff, the Man in Black, stood up to a barrage in the first half – and wasn't beaten. By comparison, my own job was a sinecure. Once I had to advance to block a shot from Glazer, through on his own; but it was Israel's solitary chance in the game. The interval brought a pep talk from Jimmy Murphy, directed mainly at the forward line: each member was spoken to, in turn.

The second half produced one-way traffic; I watched with some interest. Our shooting was better; but so was Chodoroff; who cuts out high crosses with marvellous ease, for so short a man. It was while trying to punch away a centre from Medwin that he sustained a broken nose, John Charles's elbow catching him across the face, and I'm sure the injury affected his play – our first goal occurred within minutes.

Cliff Jones, after some good work, put in a shot which was blocked but not cleared, and Ivor Allchurch screwed the ball in almost from the dead line, with twenty minutes to go.

Had Chodoroff been less dazed, I am pretty sure he would have stopped that goal.

Israel, far from trying to wipe out the goal, went back still more on defence. At one time, ten players could be counted in their penalty-box: I know, because I counted them. I was beginning to wish I had brought a good book with me. If I'd had any money on me, I would certainly have bought an ice cream from the seller behind the goal. I had enough spare time on my hands to sink a dozen cornets.

Wales' second goal simply had to come, and at last Cliff Jones cracked a square pass from Medwin into the net. Israel concentrated still further on keeping down the score – I know that they were highly delighted with their two-goal defeat, which they considered to be a moral victory. The only thing which marred their joy was that poor Chodoroff was taken to hospital in a semi-conscious state, the result of his collision with Charles. He couldn't, poor fellow, have heard the great ovation given to him by the Cardiff crowd, but by the evening he'd recovered sufficiently to send a message of good luck to us all, at the banquet.

Apparently Chodoroff is to Israel what Stan Matthews is to England. He is due to open a sports shop in Tel Aviv, and the best I can wish him is that he makes as great a success of it as he has made of keeping goal.

16
WALES GO TO SWEDEN

Without hesitation, I would say that the 1958 World Cup, with Wales, was the best trip that I have ever been on – and I have been on quite a few. In the first place, you could never hope to find a better crowd of boys, and the team spirit was absolutely great: it never wavered. As court jester, and a suitably caustic one, there was Derek Sullivan, the auburn-haired Cardiff half-back, self-appointed leader of "The Big Five", an enterprising group within the group. My own colleague, Dave Bowen, ably captained the team; Jimmy Murphy managed it with exactly the right blend of authority and good humour, and relations between the players and officials were excellent.

Added to all this, we succeeded in reaching the quarter-final round – something which neither England nor Scotland contrived to do. This was a good answer to those critics who maintained beforehand that Wales had no business in such a competition, that we not only wouldn't win a match; we would not even score a goal.

Before leaving for Stockholm, where our qualifying group with Sweden, Mexico and Hungary was to take place, the team met for five enjoyable days in London, staying at an hotel within a couple of hundred yards of the English Football Association. When on the first day we began training in Hyde Park, which stands practically opposite the hotel, we were politely told that football was not permitted. But the keeper added that in the circumstances, he was prepared to turn a blind eye and allow us to carry on with our five-a-side match. The following day there was no such complication, as we played in a practice game at the Bank of England ground, Roehampton.

The usual speeches and bouquets greeted us when we touched down at Stockholm; then we drove out to Saltsjobaden, eight miles from the city, where our headquarters were to be. The day after we had beaten Israel at Cardiff, making qualification sure, Herbert Powell, our secretary, had flown out to choose the hotel; and a very good choice he'd made. It must, indeed, have been one of the best in Sweden.

Situated on a beautiful lake, Saltsjobaden appears to be a weekend playground for the rich. Someone told us that there were four hundred yachts on that lake; I never counted them myself, but it could well have been true. Nearby there was a swimming pool, and we used it quite a lot in the first few sunny days that followed.

Our training was done on the local sports ground, in front of crowds of fascinated locals. Naturally enough, John Charles was the centre of interest when he arrived, two days later, after a long saga of will-he-won't-he involving Juventus and the Italian and Welsh F.A.

"John," said Derek Sullivan, solemnly greeting him, "you're the greatest thing that's arrived in Saltsjobaden since sliced bread."

Two practice games had been arranged for us against the local side: a good idea, I thought, remembering that the Hungarians had warmed up against little teams, before pulverizing England at Wembley. In those games we scored thirty-three goals without reply. I did suggest to Jimmy Murphy that we give them one goal for their troubles, but he just would not hear of it. Ludicrous though they were, the two games served a good purpose, if only as a confidence builder. By the time we took the field against Hungary for the first game at Sandviken, we were a team who had faith in ourselves.

Before the match, the Hungarians followed the usual continental practice of having a long warm-up period. They spent a full half-hour on the training ground opposite the stadium, and certainly it seemed to benefit them. Within four minutes, they were a goal in front.

Perhaps if we had won the toss, it would not have been scored. Just before the kick-off, I told Dave Bowen that if he should call correctly, we must play with our backs to a very low sun. As it turned out, he had no say in the matter. Incidentally, the World Cup referees adopted a very intelligent way of tossing up, especially with two sides speaking different languages. Instead of using a coin, they used a disc, one side of which was yellow and the other red. The captains did not pick their colour, but were each allotted one by the referee. Dave, as I've observed, was unlucky, and Josef Bozsik put us to face the sun.

After four minutes, Nandor Hidegkuti, playing his familiar roving centre-forward game, picked up a ball in midfield, worked it down to the edge of our area and squared it to Bozsik, who had come thundering up from right-half, in support. Bozsik, alas, was given enough time by our defence to pull the ball down and control it, before shooting into the far corner of the net from some fourteen yards. I think I might have managed to stop it, if the ball hadn't travelled into the glare of the sun.

The Hungarians, I thought, would now settle down to play some football. Instead, they started rough stuff. John Charles especially was on the wrong end of some very violent tackling. Every time he got the ball he was tackled by two Hungarian defenders – usually from behind. These methods never allowed us to play football as we wanted to; instead, we too began to play hard, but as the game wore on, we steadily began to get on top. John Charles equalized, soaring characteristically high in the air to a corner by Cliff Jones. Gyula Grosics, in goal, seemed to think that the ball was going wide. At all events, he made no effort to save it, but stood there while it crept just inside the post.

For the next fifteen minutes we slung everything at the Hungarians without being able to increase our tally, but there were no more goals in the game. Hungary came nearest to scoring soon after the restart, when Hidegkuti hit a ball on the volley from eight yards out. Stuart Williams, thank goodness, blocked the ball on the line and cleared. In next day's match reports, however, I got the credit for an astonishing save! Obviously, the view from the stand wasn't a good one....

Thus the game was drawn 1-1, but I shall always maintain that we should have left the field as winners, from a penalty kick. Ivor Allchurch was through on his own when he was pulled down from behind by the full-back, Matray – with no consequences.

Hungary, deprived of Kocsis, Puskas and Czibor, weren't even a shadow of the team which hammered England at Wembley, a criticism that applied on the day to two of that team's stars, Grosics and Hidegkuti. Bozsik, on the other hand, seemed to have worn much better. With forwards Tichy and Sandor, I thought him the best of the side.

After that encouraging start, we continued to enjoy Saltsjobaden. There were the occasional problems with language, of course: it wouldn't have been a foreign tour without them. Ivor Allchurch, arriving thirstily back in the hotel after a morning's training, telephoned room service for two lemonades. After three-quarters of an hour had gone by, he gave it up as a bad job, and went to lunch. On returning to his room, he found two plates of bacon and eggs awaiting him.

There were nautical adventures, too. Walking along the quayside in search of a boat, Colin Webster, John Charles and I at last found a man who'd hire one to us for ten kroner an hour. First, however, we had to convince him that one of us could handle such a boat. Colin Webster earnestly assured him there no better man for the job than he. The owner started the engine, pushed us out, and Colin, every inch a seaman, took charge. We hadn't gone ten yards when we met the first hazard – a yacht – which we cleared by a matter of inches. Clear of the other boats, we now settled down for a pleasant hour – when suddenly the engine failed.

For half an hour, the three of us worked on it without success, while on the quayside the owner waved frantic arms at us, summoning us in. There was only one way out, and that was to row. But of Colin claimed to be an experienced helmsman, he made no claims at all when it came to rowing. That job, alas, was mine, and it turned out to be a long one. When at last we reached the owner and the quay, we had quite a job trying to get our kroner back. We succeeded at last, the owner leaving us with the kindly thought that if ever we wanted to hire another boat, he'd be delighted to see us go elsewhere.

Some of the boys went to the Tivoli Fairground in Stockholm. On his return to the hotel, all we could get out of one of them was that he'd never seen so many beautiful women, but he couldn't understand why they were all accompanied by rather dreary looking men, most of whom seemed to be wearing glasses.

"I know where I'm going in the morning," one of our comedians promptly said.

"Where?" asked someone else.

"To the opticians", was the reply, "to get some glasses."

While we were in Saltsjobaden, we met three English lads who had hitch-hiked from Coventry, just to see the World Cup games. Two of them worked at the hotel as waiters; they'd obtained a work permit by saying they were students, who could speak the Welsh language. The third, more conventionally, had tried to get a job at his own trade and had been turned down, which meant he was dependent on the others, who smuggled food out of the hotel to him.

One day, he told me, he was nearly caught in the hotel grounds. He'd been given some food by his friends, and had stealthily climbed a tree to eat it. Settling comfortably on one of the branches to enjoy the meal, he suddenly noticed one of the hotel staff coming straight towards him. In haste, he climbed farther up the tree, till he was out of sight. He lost his meal – but nobody caught him.

After Hungary – Mexico, and this was a match we felt sure we would win. Indeed, it was probably over-confidence which prevented us from doing so. Mexico were by general consent the poorest team in the competition. In the event, they turned out to be a very hard side to play against: such was their fitness that they attacked with ten men and defended with ten! Every man in the side seemed to be a ball player, and we simply could make no headway; it took us a full half-hour to score a goal, through Ivor Allchurch.

That was that, I thought, for Mexicans staying at our hotel had told me that if we scored one, we'd score a hatful. But the hatful never came. Two minutes from time, in fact, a wing to wing movement split our defence, and the unmarked Belmonte headed home from inside-right, thus atoning for a chance missed earlier in the game.

The Mexicans, I thought, were cry-babies: after a good, hard tackle they would actually lie on the ground and burst into tears. By contrast, their exhibition when they scored was one of delirium. Every Mexican player was in our six-yard box jumping on Belmonte, with goalkeeper Carbajal haring downfield to join in like a Mexican McDonald Bailey.

We were a shocking side that day, but there was consolation the day after when we saw Sweden beat Hungary

2-1 at the Rasunda Stadium. This meant that a draw against Sweden, would probably qualify us for a play-off with Hungary. That Sunday, once more in the Rasunda, whose rich turf is as exhausting as Wembley, we got that point, though it must have been an abysmal game to watch. Sweden, who'd already qualified, put in five reserves, while we planned that John Charles should play up-field for the first quarter of an hour, in hopes of an early goal, then drop back to a virtual centre-half position. We got our goalless draw, and we were still unbeaten: we had not won a game either.

Since our match at the Rasunda started at two o'clock, we were forced to wait several hours before hearing that Hungary, as expected, had crushed Mexico, and would meet us in a play-off.

Taking the field against them for the second time, in a Rasunda Stadium which contained merely two thousand spectators, we knew we were through should we beat them this time, though we weren't going to repeat our mistake of over-confidence.

Hungary again started as the better side, and again they scored first: this time, however, it took them twenty-seven minutes. Tichy, standing on the corner of the six-yard box, hit the ball hard and low inside the near post.

In the second half, Hungary resumed their strong arm methods. Three times John Charles was pulled down in the penalty area while going up for crosses. Every member of the crowd thought these three clear penalties, but not M. Latyshev, the Russian referee. Earlier in this book I have praised him, but in my view he was another, lesser man on this day's showing.

When we did equalize, it was one of the finest goals I have ever seen. Ivor Allchurch, who had a magnificent tour, crashed a forty-yard pass by John Charles past Grosics on the full volley – from outside the penalty area. The goalkeeper had no chance of saving.

Now we began to put on pressure, and the Hungarians were at full stretch to keep us at bay. Five minutes after the Allchurch goal, however, their defence buckled again, and this time the goal was a present. Grosics rolled a goal kick out to Sarosi, who pushed the ball back to him. Terry Medwin, however, had anticipated the move. He nipped in from the wing, and had the ball in the net before Grosics could touch it.

Naturally enough the Hungarians were distressed by this. Though we could not understand what they were saying, it was impossible not to hear that they were arguing among themselves, and we knew we'd beaten them, now that we had them so rattled. We decided, however, to adopt our "Swedish" policy of bringing John Charles back in defence, to prevent a possible equalizer.

With John and the two wing halves playing a negative game, our attacks were reduced to the odd breakaway, and in one of these an unpleasant incident took place. Ron Hewitt, our inside-right, beat Sipos, the Hungarian centre-half, who apparently resented it. He took a savage swing at Hewitt, catching him on the knee, and the Cardiff man went down hard, to be carried off on a stretcher. Sipos was rightly sent off the field.

Yet there was still some kick left in the Hungarians. In the next minute, Matray chipped a ball beautifully over the defensive wall from a free kick to Fenyvesi, running in. The winger got his head to the ball, which soared for the far corner of the net. Throwing myself desperately sideways, I managed to get a hand to it, and push it round the post for a corner. This we cleared – and the whistle blew for time. We were in the quarter-finals. Little Wales had confounded all their critics.

And so we left Saltsjobaden for Gothenburg, where we were to meet the favourites, Brazil. There were tears from the youngsters in the local cafe, where we had swigged Coca-Cola and played records in the evenings. Kungalv, a little town outside Gothenburg, was dull by comparison.

For this match, any luck we may have had deserted us. John Charles was ruled unfit to play. Certainly we had everything to gain and nothing to lose, but where was our striking power? We had heard much about Brazil's fine display against the Russians, who had been demoralized by the wizardry of Garrincha, an outside-right whose name means "little bird". In the middle of the attack we faced the young Mazzola, a nineteen-year-old who'd just joined Milan at a fabulous signing-on fee. Then there was Didi, the black magician at inside-right.

We didn't disgrace ourselves. Starting as underdogs was much to our advantage; we always seemed to prefer it that way. Certainly Brazil were the better side that cool evening, but our defence played a clever funnelling, retreating game, and most of Brazil's shooting was confined to long range. Once Garrincha, who was generally subdued by Mel Hopkins and Dave Bowen, blasted in a shot from close range, but I managed to hold it cleanly. Chewing gum helped; I've acquired the habit of rubbing it on my hands before the game, so that it causes the ball to stick.

If only Big John had been playing, I think we might have beaten the Brazilians. It was ironical that in this game, when he wasn't there in the middle with his formidable head, our wingers crossed more high centres than in any other match. As it was, the only goal came twenty minutes from time, when the coloured Pele hooked the ball over his head, shot for goal, and the ball struck Stuart William's outstretched foot and sneaked past me into the corner. He and Mel Charles, in the centre-half position, had played heroically, and we all came off the field feeling quite pleased with the result. After all, we'd played a hard game only two days before, and we had still put up a better showing against Brazil than Russia.

Among our regrets was one that we would have picked up another £100 match fee for the semi-final, if we had won, with the final also in prospect. Nevertheless, it was a heartening tour. What players do I best remember? Night and day: the flaxen-haired Nacka Skoglund of Sweden and the coal-black Didi of Brazil. Skoglund didn't extend himself against Wales, but I still thought him the best Swedish player, on what I saw; a brilliant, fragile ball player with a splendid swerve. Didi is the master strategist, the brain behind Brazil. He swerves the ball bewilderingly with the outside of his right foot and seems to have mastered every pass in the game, both short and long. Tichy, the Hungarian inside-forward, looked a good player, too. He gave me some very hard shots to save, and he scored a lovely, long-range goal against Sweden.

In our own team, I was happy enough with my form after some difficult games at the end of the league season. Stuart Williams created a great impression at right-back with his tackling and his calm distribution: the Pressman who mistook me for Stuart told me he thought I was the best full-back in the world.

John Charles, I thought, was not what the Swedish crowds had expected him to be, but perhaps they were asking too much from him in so tough a competition; a competition which left the Welsh team looking ahead to the future with new confidence and hope.

Also available from GCR Books:

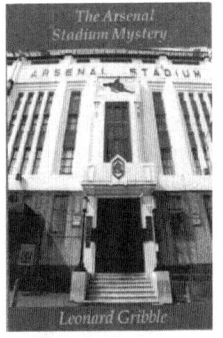

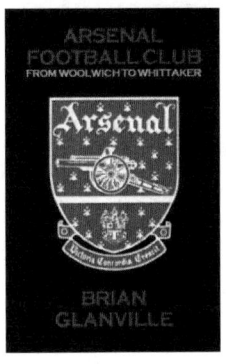

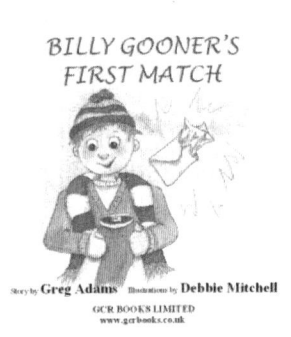

BILLY GOONER'S FIRST MATCH
Story by **Greg Adams** Illustrations by **Debbie Mitchell**
GCR BOOKS LIMITED
www.gcrbooks.co.uk

Visit **www.gcrbooks.co.uk** for details.

ARSENAL INDEPENDENT SUPPORTERS' ASSOCIATION

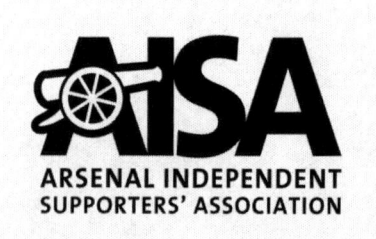

AISA was formed on Sunday 1st October 2000, hours before Thierry Henry's 'wonder goal' at Highbury that led to a 1-0 victory over Manchester United. Over 50 supporters attended the inaugural meeting at St. Paul's Road, London N1. **AISA**'s membership, including associate members, has since grown to over 8,000, making it by far the largest Arsenal supporters club.

The main objects of **AISA** are to:

- Represent and campaign on behalf of Arsenal supporters.
- Organise high quality services for **AISA** members.
- Promote the history, values and traditions of Arsenal Football Club.
- Encourage the Directors and Management of Arsenal Football Club to appreciate, welcome and value the support and participation of all Arsenal fans.

AISA believes that fans' views and experiences should be at the centre of the Club's decision-making process. We work co-operatively with other Arsenal supporters organisations to keep supporters' views at the forefront.

AISA campaigns on issues such as improving the atmosphere, providing better catering arrangements, the stewarding and policing operations, transport to and from the stadium. We meet regularly with the Club's chief executive, and with various other Arsenal senior managers and directors.

Everything we do is informed by our members, through their feedback, and by fans in general through regular surveys and various other formal and informal tools.

AISA has developed a charity fundraising programme, mainly supporting the Arsenal charity of the season, which has raised over £70,000 in the last 5 years.

Following the 2011 change in the ownership of the Club we continue to campaign against debt being secured against the club and the raising of short-term profits through significant increases in ticket prices.

AISA has a number of important relationships with external organisations, notably Islington Borough Council and the Islington Police as well as Delaware North, Arsenal's catering supplier.

Every Arsenal supporter is welcome to join AISA. We have members as young as 8 and others well into their 80s. Many members attend matches every week, others are not so lucky but support the team in every way they can. AISA is based in Islington but our members live in every part of the UK, and in over 40 other countries.

Membership fees are minimal; join at www.aisa.org or write to AISA, PO Box 65011, London N5 9AX. For more information email us at info@aisa.org.

The Arsenal Supporters' Trust exists to bring together Shareholders and Supporters of Arsenal Football Club.

Our goal is to ensure an element of supporter ownership, representation and influence is maintained at Arsenal in the years ahead. Large numbers of our members are already shareholders.

In August 2010 Arsenal Fanshare was launched to facilitate mutual ownership of Arsenal shares.
www.arsenalfanshare.com

Every member of the Trust shares in ownership of Arsenal Football Club through the shares the Trust owns.

The Trust works with its members, Arsenal executives, the club's Board, major shareholders and other Arsenal supporter groups to help build Arsenal into a world class sporting institution.

Arsenal is a name and a club already widely admired around the football world. Together we can take it to even greater heights, both on and off the field. The Arsenal tradition is one of ground-breaking innovation. Please join us and support our work.

As well as holding monthly board meetings which members are welcome to attend, the Trust holds special events for its membership. In recent seasons, these have included an annual Q&A session with the managing director/CEO of the club, a Christmas drinks social in Arsenal's exclusive Diamond Club, a tour of the stadium's press facilities and a meeting for members with relevant ministers at the Houses of Parliament.

For details of how to join, visit our website at
www.arsenaltrust.org